Nurturing the Courage
of
Pilgrims

follow-up reflective and spiritual exercises
for
A Pilgrimage to the Land of the Saints

Prepared by Timothy J. Ray

Dedicated to the Memory
of
Bertha Salazar, MMB
Spiritual Foster-Mother and Soul Friend

Table of Contents

Preface

nurturing a holistic spirituality

If you are reading this, you have made quite an impressive – and hopefully rewarding – spiritual journey. At the same time, you understand that that journey has not ended and you are hoping to find further guidance and assistance as you move forward. It is in that hope, that the reflections and exercises of this booklet were prepared.

In both Celtic and Ignatian spirituality (the primary spiritual sources for *A Journey to the Land of the Saints* and *A Pilgrimage to the Land of the Saints*), faith is not only a matter of personal piety. In both of these great spiritual traditions, prayer creates a deepening relationship with God – allowing the person to know the fullness of God's love and forgiveness – and invites each man or woman to find his or her unique way of helping to build God's kingdom. This fosters a dynamic spiritual life in which your prayer and spiritual disciplines interact with the requirements of our "citizenship" in heaven and the impulses to share our faith with others as our love for God overflows to those around us. The ancient Celtic saints referred to this dynamic and multifaceted approach to faith as becoming "colonies of heaven".

The relationships within this understanding of spirituality may be demonstrated with the following diagram:

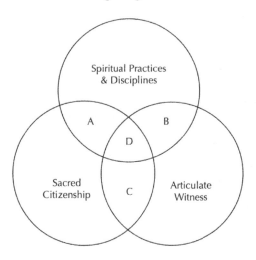

A = Ideals — seeing a vision of possibilities
B = Language — hearing a voice of hope
C = Advocacy — speaking truth to power
D = Place of Resurrection — manifesting the Kingdom

In this holistic approach, the three primary aspects of a life of faith (or spirituality) – spiritual practices and disciplines, sacred citizenship (the ways in which our faith requires us to behave toward others as fellow children of God) and articulate witness (the impulse to share our experience of God's love with others) – interact to give you insight and guidance as you strive to respond to God's love with courage and consistency.

Of these three components of a spiritual life, the most important is your devotion to the spiritual practices and disciplines that nurture a mutual relationship of love between you and God. Without this loving bond, the rest of your spiritual life will quickly wither. However, both your fulfillment of the responsibilities of sacred citizenship and your ability to respond to the invitation to articulate witness helps sustain your life of prayer by making your faith tangible and by reminding you of the need you have for God's continuing support.

Ultimately, however, the interplay between these three aspects of the spiritual life offers the direction you need to find and fulfill your ultimate purpose in God's plan. When your prayer embraces the challenges of sacred citizenship, you see the possibilities of God's kingdom and embrace the ideals that allow you to act in the world with justice and compassion. Similarly, when your love for God invites you to offer witness and you bring these desires prayer, you discover the language you need to express hope to others. Finally, when you feel called to give witness to God's love as a "citizen of heaven", God provides you with the words to speak truth to power and the tools to advocate for a more just world.

With consistent prayer and discernment, these seemingly distinct but interconnected ingredients in the spiritual life converge to reveal the place or ministry that best allows you to give hope-filled witness to God's love to those around you in the world. This is the modern equivalent of what the ancient Celtic saints called the "place of resurrection". It is the place that has been prepared for you, in which you live in the love and joy God while creating a "colony of heaven".

Whether explicitly stated or implied, the reflections and exercises of this booklet seeks to provide opportunities for you to explore these aspects of your spiritual life – and to discern the connections between them – so you may discover the path to your own "place of resurrection".

Using these Exercises

The reflective and spiritual exercises in this collection were developed as the follow-up to the retreat in *A Pilgrimage to the Land of the Saints*, so there are numerous references to that experience and its practices throughout this book. Still, while they are enriched by the experiences of the retreat, the exercises collected in this book remain independent spiritual activities. However, you will need to ignore the references to the retreat found in this book and focus your attention on the instructions for the reflections and prayers.

Most of the exercises in this book are self-explanatory and easy to engage with no prior experience of *A Pilgrimage to the Land of the Saints* but the scriptural prayers suggested in various parts of this collection rely on Ignatian forms of prayer used during the retreat (e.g, imaginative contemplation, the application of the senses, etc.). If you are not familiar with these styles of prayer, you will find resources to help you at:

http://www.resources.silentheron.net

These include suggestions for creating a sacred space for prayer, some rituals for entering that space, step-by-step instructions in imaginative contemplation (and a variation called the application of the senses), two considerations of the events of your day (called examens) and an online audio course on Ignatian prayers styles. If you need to learn these techniques of imaginative prayer, you should take time to practice them before approaching the exercises in this collection.

Finally, as you engage these reflective and spiritual exercises, you should use a notebook to prepare for each prayer exercise and then – after reviewing the thoughts and emotions evoked during your prayer – record your experiences in some type of a journal. These serve different purposes and should not be combined into one item. The notebook will help you prepare and organize for prayer, while the journal will preserve your memories of the prayers and their effect upon you.

Acknowledgements

Richard King's image of Ita on the cover of this booklet is used with the permission of *The Capuchin Annual* and the King estate.

"Ita and the Thirst for Holiness" is an excerpt from Johnston McMaster's *A Passion for Justice: Social Ethics in the Celtic Tradition* (Edinburgh: Dunedin Academic Press Ltd., 2008) and used with the permission of the author.

The excerpts in "Ita and the Virtue of Simplicity" are from Gabriel Cooper Rochelle's *A Staff to the Pilgrim: Meditations on the Way with Nine Celtic Saints* (Emmaus, PA: Golden Alley Press, 2016) and used with the permission of the author.

The stories in the three sections of "Nurturing the Courage of Pilgrims" and in "Sacred Citizenship and the Challenge of Hope" are from Edward C. Sellner's *Wisdom of the Celtic* Saints (Notre Dame, IN: Ave Maria Press, 1993).

The morning and evening prayers in the three sections of 'Nurturing the Courage of Pilgrims' were developed with permission from prayers collected in Paul Stratman's *Prayers from the Ancient Celtic Church* (Scotts Valley, CA: CreateSpace Independent Publishing Platform, 2018).

The poem "My Speech" in the evening prayer "Life be in my speech, sense in what I say", "Articulate Witness & the Virtue of Hospitality" and "Seeking Your Place of Resurrection" as well as the poem "Grant me tears, O Lord" in "Preparing a Personal Penitential" are from Oliver Davies' and Thomas O'Loughlin's *Celtic Spirituality* (New York: Paulist Press, 1999).

The traditional Scottish prayers presented in "Preparing a Personal Penitential" are from Alexander Carmichael's *Carmina Gadelica* (Edinburgh: Floris Books, 1994).

Finally, all biblical citations are from the New Revised Standard Version of the Bible (New York: Harper Collins, 1989), used with the permission of the US National Council of churches.

Ita: the foster mother of saints

Considerations

The exercises of this section expand on your retreat experiences during "(I) Barrind's Story" in A Pilgrimage to the Land of the Saints. *Before proceeding to the following reflections and prayers, it might be helpful to review "Walking with the Celtic Saints" following "(I) Barrind's Story" in the first section of* A Journey to the Land of the Saints.

In *A Journey to the Land of the Saints* and *A Pilgrimage to the Land of the Saints*, you traveled with Brendan on his adventures and discovered the aspects of your own adventurous spirituality you shared with him. In the reflections and exercises of this booklet, you will take time to hear the voice of the woman who raised Brendan from childhood and whose spiritual counsel Brendan sought throughout his life – Ita of Kileedy. While she never traveled abroad like her famous foster-son, Ita traversed an adventurous spiritual landscape through her interior life of prayerful discernment and through her devoted service to those around her in God's name.

This section will introduce you to Ita and her spiritual significance so you may hear her more clearly in the subsequent reflections and exercises.

Note: While this section (and the ones that follow) offer suggestions for your consideration as you approach these exercises, you should proceed at your own pace in a spirit of prayerful openness. However, while you may find it useful to spend more time with the exercises than suggested, you may diminish their impact and value if you try to go through them too quickly. So, trust in God's presence and guidance as you move forward – especially when you feel challenged by an exercise and its requirements – and you will find the rhythm that best meets your needs.

Before beginning this section:

You should review your retreat journal to see if there are any significant periods of prayer during the first day/week addressed in this section.

Take your time and enjoy the memories of your retreat experience, bringing into your consciousness any particular graces or insights you received from your earlier prayers. If you repeated any of these prayers during the interval between your retreat and now, reflect upon these repetitions and observe any differences between these two (or more) experiences with regard to content or emotional energy. Afterward, write your observations in your journal.

You should also reread the reflections for the first day/week in the first section of A Journey to the Land of the Saints. Consider your initial answers the review questions and exercises at the end of the reading, reflecting on how these answers may have changed during the months since you first engaged them. If you did not complete these review questions and exercises earlier, take time to consider them now in a deliberate and contemplative manner. Again, write your observations in your journal.

Reading the selections in this section:

After this period of review, when you are ready, begin by reading Johnston MacMaster's reflection on Ita slowly and in a contemplative manner, discerning any connections you feel between it and the prayers of your retreat. Then read in an equally reflective manner the questions that follow the selection, deciding if there are any questions you might want to answer together.

Then, on separate days, approach each question (or cluster of questions). Begin by asking God's help in understanding the value of Ita's spiritual tenets in your own life. Afterward, reread the question slowly and note any significant phrases or words in it before answering the question and recording it in your journal. It is important that you take as much time as you want (or feel you need) in answering each question, even if this means extending the process and spending more than one day on a particular issue or concern.

    Note: You might find it helpful to imagine yourself answering the question(s) in the presence of Jesus, speaking with him about the nuances of the question(s) and your responses to them.

After completing your consideration of the selection by Johnston MacMaster, devote a prayer session to reflectively address the questions after each of the selections from Gabriel Cooper Rochelle. Begin by asking God to reveal the graces you will need to fully appreciate the spiritual value of Ita's spirituality in your life. Then, in a reflective and prayerful manner, read Gabriel Cooper Rochelle's observation and answer the questions that follow it. Again, it is important that you take as much time as you want (or need) in answering the questions.

An excerpt from Johnston McMaster's
A Passion for Justice: social ethics in the Celtic tradition

Johnston McMaster was lecturer and co-ordinator of the Education for Reconciliation program at the Irish School of Ecumenics in Belfast. His areas of interest and on-going research include reconciliation and peacebuilding, Celtic Christianity and spirituality, social ethics and inter-faith dialogue.

Ita's name is said to be derived from IOTA, thirst. She became Ita because of her thirst for holiness. It may well be that it was this quality of life that drew many foster children to Kileedy and which also attracted so many women.

> "St Brendan once asked what were the three works most pleasing to God, and the three works most displeasing to him. Ita answered, "Three things that please God most are true faith in God with a pure heart, a simple life with a grateful spirit, and generosity inspired by charity. The three things that most displease God are a mouth that hates people, a heart harboring resentments, and confidence in wealth."

Holiness has to do with wholeness of living, and there is a rich holistic spirituality about Ita's response. The ethics of holiness portrayed here are essentially relational. It is in relationship to God, others and the world that faith is lived with integrity. "A mouth that hates people" is speech that is bitter and destructive of other people. When characters and reputations are destroyed by words there is a hate motive behind it. Conflict is not only created by prejudiced and malicious words, but also words kill. People may claim not to have broken the law by destroying property or people's lives but incitement to hate or opposition has often been taken to its logical conclusion by others. Sectarianism, racism and homophobia work that way.

"A heart harboring resentments" is self-destructive as well as destructive of relationships. It produces a bitterness that poisons feelings and attitudes and imprisons one in anger and self-pity. The inner spirit of resentment and negativity blocks the ability to relate, not only to the immediate other but also to all others. One engages in battle with oneself and other persons.

"Confidence in wealth" is misplaced trust. Life becomes centred on accumulation, getting more and eventually on greed. It is the insatiable desire for more which often convinces itself that scarcity is the perennial problem. There is not enough, which can be behind personal pursuit of success and plenty, as well as motivate imperial expansionism; more weapons, gold, land, oil. Wealth is usually gained at the expense of others. Life centered on wealth and more wealth often shuts out the poorer neighbour and diminishes compassion.

Ita's positive values enhance relationships and help build a caring and compassionate community.

"True faith in God with a pure heart" is the authentic centre and focus of confidence. Commitment to and confidence in God is to centre life and shape relationality by God's values of love, mercy, justice and compassion. The pure heart is not moral perfection, the Celtic saints were down to Earth and all too human. It is, as Jesus taught in the Beatitudes, the single-minded commitment to the life of God in the world, the blessedness of the merciful, justice seekers and peacemakers. The pure in heart, committed to these values and praxis, see God and or know God. And to know God is to build a merciful, just and peaceful community.

"A simple life with a grateful spirit" is a way of life with integrity. A consumerist society imposing on us its liturgy of advertising, creating need and necessity when they are not really required, produces a life-spirit of insatiable desire. It creates an endless competition between people, a lifestyle of jealousy, envy and covetousness. Neighbor is set against neighbor, child against child, and humans against the earth. Western lifestyle is unsustainable at the expense of the rest of humanity and the ecological systems. Ita knew nothing of our contemporary environmental crisis, but she practiced simplicity of living. She only accepted small grants of land for her foundations and she was committed to the poor and the marginalized. Simplicity of lifestyle is a faith commitment for the twenty-first century. It is holiness in action, and a grateful spirit is the opposite of a grasping spirit.

"Generosity inspired by charity" is Ita's third positive value towards others. At the heart of this practice is compassion. One story describes a hospice-like ministry which cares for a dying abbot, who perhaps like all humans facing their mortality has anxieties and fears. Because of Ita's caring and compassion "Saint Comhganus then left this world accompanied by choirs of angels".

In another story Ita shows tremendous compassion for a murderer who seeks forgiveness and reconciliation. Ita held together justice and mercy, which not all can do, and saw justice as ultimately restorative and transformative. Ita was not prepared to leave another human to "rot in hell" or to "lock him up and throw away the key". In yet another story she responded with compassion and patience to a man whose ways she had wanted to change. He was wounded in a battle against west Munster and she sent a messenger to him. "He brought the brother back to Ita who received him kindly, and he was healed of his wounds. Later, he did a fitting penance, according to Ita's order, and died a happy death".

Caring, healing, forgiveness and reconciliation, restorative justice and transformation of relationships and life were all qualities practiced in Ita's foundation at Kileedy. Her response to Brendan articulated her thirst for holiness and expressed the essence of holiness. It was not an other-worldly piety but a centredness on God which was a generous ethical relationality.

In a reflective manner, take time to prayerfully consider these questions and record your observations in your journal:

1.   Remember that Brendan asked this question as an adult. What does this tell you about the relationship between Ita and Brendan? Do you have a person in your life with whom you share this level of trust? Does this person have the depth of spirituality to be a true soul friend? What do you bring to this person in your relationship?

2.   How do the three sinful behaviors help you understand the virtuous ones?

3.   How do the actions pleasing – and those displeasing – to God illuminate the holistic spirituality of the ancient Celtic saints? How do they illuminate your spirituality and faith?

4.   Which of the action(s) described by Ita as being displeasing to God challenges you in your own life and prayer? Does Ita offer you any guidance in addressing this (or these) challenges?

5.   Which of the action(s) described by Ita as being pleasing to God challenges you in your own life and prayer? Does Ita offer you any support in nurturing this (or these) qualities?

6.   How does Brendan's question for Ita help you understand the "community of saints"? Do you participate in that community? If so, how? If not, why not? Does the word "saint" frighten or encourage you?

7.   How does Ita's response to Brendan help you understand the presence of God in yourself?… In others?… In the world around you? What does it teach you about seeing (and listening for) God's activity in your daily life?… In your interactions with others?… In your actions on behalf of God's creatures, both human and nonhuman?

If a particular question seems especially significant, write your response in your journal.

Excerpts from Gabriel Cooper Rochelle's
A Staff to the Pilgrim: Meditations on the Way
with Nine Celtic Saints

Gabriel Cooper Rochelle is an Orthodox priest. He has written extensively and conducted workshops in Celtic Christian spirituality. His formal studies in Celtic Studies at University of Wales Trinity Saint David focused on the Welsh tradition but he also explored other areas, especially the richness of the Irish traditions.

Consider the following selections and answer their companion questions:

God is not the reward of our search for God. *God is present in all of life, and it is our task to discover God. Spiritual disciplines can unblock the channels of communication and vision between us: communication, because we lose the ability to hear God in the din and roar of our own inner chatter and the words the world hurls at us, and vision, because we lose the ability to see God's Presence in a world where pain mingles with pleasure and suffering with joy.*

Prayer, fasting, and other disciplines are means to experience God through our senses once again.

1.   What spiritual practices and disciplines have you found most helpful in discerning the presence of God in your life and in the world around you? Which have you found challenging or unhelpful? What have these experiences taught you about yourself?

2.   How has your experiences of spiritual practices and disciplines changed over the course of your life? Which, if any, have retained their vitality throughout your life and which have you discarded over time? Why?

9

The spiritual life begins and ends in poverty. *In some senses this is another word for simplicity as over against duplicity. Saints like Ita are models of simplicity; their lack of guile is astonishing. They show us that we stand impoverished before God, with no riches to offer to buy the presence of God. Our poverty is, on the other hand, the major asset we bring before God, insofar as we acknowledge and reflect on it. We cannot own the riches of God; they must come as gift. For us to be gifted, we must recognize how poor we are: "Blessed are the poor in spirit, for theirs is the kingdom of heaven."*

We are poor in many ways:
— because we move toward death, and nothing can buy us life
— because we are unique, and nothing can buy us the life another person leads; we must learn to accept our own lives and ourselves as we are
— because we are needy, and nothing can buy us out of need for the natural, material, and human resources by which we live
— because we have limits, and nothing can expand those limits; we were born in a particular time of particular parents with a particular heritage and particular physical limitations which become more evident are we grow older
— because we are vulnerable, and to become more fully human we must increase our vulnerability by loving.

1.   Of the forms of poverty listed in the selection, which do you find most challenging to accept? Which do you find the easiest to accept? How have these different types of poverty shaped your spiritual life? Be specific as possible.

2.   How is your human poverty enriched by God's action in your life? How does it open you to God's many gifts?... To other people in your life?... To the situations you face in life, both good and bad?

The spiritual life calls us to recognize and live with our poverty. *It is only by accepting our poverty that we learn to live in history and stop imagining fantasy lives in which we "escape history."*

Our poverty becomes an asset when it becomes simplicity. Simplicity does not mean simplemindedness. It means, first of all, the opposite of duplicity. Duplicity means that we operate with a host of different agenda items, rather than to realize and embrace what the Danish theologian Søren Kierkegaard offers: "Purity of heart is to will one thing."

We must avoid all multiplicity of motives as we approach God with but one motive that may be expressed in several ways: "What is the will of God for my life?" or "How may I give glory to God through my living?" or "How can I will just one thing?" Prayer centers on seeking the answers to these questions.

Simplicity may also mean freedom from artificiality. Saints like Ita exhibit the purity which we seek to manifest in our own lives, though we so often fall short.

1.   How does simplicity help you become a child of God? How does it help you see and hear God in your life more clearly? How does it help you follow God's guidance more freely? How does it help you reflect God's presence in the world more fully? Be specific as possible.

2.   What are your greatest challenges when trying to attain simplicity of spirit?… And of life? What do these challenges teach you about yourself?… And your openness to being a child of God?… And your resistance to being a child of God?

Simplicity directs us to be attentive to the here-and-now, to cut off our frustrating worry or fretting about the future and our endless recitation of the past. *Simplicity calls us to live "just as I am, without one plea." To this end we seek prayer.*

Prayer begins and ends in silence. It begins with our silence in the presence of God and ends with our presence in the silence of God.

All prayer rests on the prior word of God which emerges out of the silence – God has "spoken" to the world in creation, in the act of love in Christ, and through the Spirit. Prayer is one response to that word, whether alone or in community. Through prayer our poverty and our simplicity are both affirmed and transformed, and the spiritual life is born.

11

1. How does your poverty and simplicity of life ground you in the present? How do these qualities help you understand yourself better? How do these qualities help you make decisions rooted in your true identity before God?

2. What role does prayer play in helping you embrace poverty and simplicity in your life?... In your relationship with God? Do you create spaces of silence stillness in your daily life so you may hear God's words and see God's actions more clearly?

St Ita, patron saint of both simplicity and blessing, taught us to thank God for the grace of the ordinary. *To thank God for the presence of those who enhance the ordinariness of our lives. To thank God for the small issues we deal with from day to day, from crabgrass to crabby relatives, from school deadlines and candy sales to job hassles. Let us not make idols of the extraordinary, because when we do, we lose sight of the One who is seen veiled through the ordinary. Let us not forget to bless the ordinary gifts and people who grace our lives.*

1. How do you find God's presence in the ordinary aspects of your day-to-day life? Do these things and events manifest God's presence easily?... Or must you search for them?

2. Do you express your gratitude for God's presence in your day-to-day life?... How? Do you reciprocate God's generosity with acts of gratitude toward God? Do you share that gratitude with others through concrete words and actions?

[The] Celtic monastic tradition which she [Ita] embodied was able to see depth in the midst of surface, simplicity in the midst of complexity, and the divine in the midst of the human. *This vision of simplicity breathed lifeblood into the Celtic tradition, and can do so again for us in our age.*

1. How is your poverty and simplicity of spirit enriched by your awareness of God's manifold activity in you?... In others?... In the world around you? Do you enrich the world through your own presence?

2.   Does your awareness of God's activity in the world differ from that of the ancient Celtic saints? What spiritual experiences of the ancient Celtic saints do you hope to emulate in your life? How will you share these moments with others?

Remember... If a particular question seems especially significant, write your response in your journal.

Nurturing the Courage of Pilgrims

Considerations

The following sections are meant to help you reflect upon the three qualities Ita believed pleased to God: true faith in God with a pure heart, a simple life with a grateful spirit, and generosity inspired by charity. Ita embodied these qualities in her personal life and in her guidance of others, but she also recognized the need for them to be reaffirmed on a daily basis so they might become – and remain -- an intrinsic and natural aspect of a person's spiritual as well as social life. So, with this in mind, these materials are presented in a manner intended to help them become habitual aspects of your prayer and interaction with others.

Like the readings in the first section, the reflection exercises and prayers presented in the following sections relate directly to aspects of your retreat. These relationships are stated at the beginning of each section so that you will be able to review your earlier experiences before engaging in the actual activities of the section.

Before approaching each subsection:

So, with this in mind, you should review your retreat journal as you did in the first section to see if there are any significant periods of prayer during the days/weeks addressed in each of the following subsections. If so, take some time to enjoy the memories of your retreat experience and the particular graces or insights you received from your earlier prayers. If you repeated any of these prayers during the interval between your retreat and now, reflect upon these repetitions and note any differences between these two (or more) experiences with regard to content or emotional energy. Afterward, write your observations in your journal.

Again, as in the previous section, you should also reread the reflections for the relevant days/weeks in the first section of A Journey to the Land of the Saints. Consider your initial answers the review questions and exercises at the end of these readings, reflecting on how these answers may have changed during the months since you first approached them. If you did not complete these review questions and exercises earlier, take time to consider them now in a contemplative manner. Again, write your observations in your journal.

Engaging the activities of each subsection:

After this review, when you are ready, begin by reading the story about Ita at the beginning of each subsection and answering the questions that follow it.

Note: The amount of time you devote to reading and reflecting upon the story and its subsequent questions should be the same has the imaginative contemplations that follow them.

When you are ready, begin by reading the story slowly and in a contemplative manner, discerning any connections you feel between it and the prayers of your retreat. Then read in an equally contemplative manner the questions that follow the story, deciding if there are any questions you might want to answer together. Finally, record in your journal any insights or observations you might have about the story as well as any graces you might request as you consider Ita's virtues.

Then, on separate days, reflectively approach each question (or cluster of questions). Begin by asking God's help in understanding the fullness of Ita's virtue and in embodying that virtue in your life. Afterward, reread the question slowly and note any significant phrases or words in it before answering the question and recording it in your journal. It is important that you take as much time as you want (or feel you need) in answering each question, even if this means extending the process and spending more than one day on a particular issue or concern.

Note: Again, as with your reflections on the readings in the first section, you might find it helpful to imagine yourself answering the question in the presence of Jesus, speaking with him about the nuances of the question(s) and your responses to them.

After completing your consideration of the questions, devote a prayer session to reflectively reviewing your answers. Ask God to reveal the graces you will need to ask for when you proceed to the imaginative contemplations. Then, read the scriptural verses presented for contemplation and decide the order in which you would like to contemplate them -- beginning with the biblical verse that seems most relevant to your current situation. If you do not feel led to organize the biblical verses in a particular manner, place them in a random order before beginning your contemplations.

Approach the biblical verses over the course of nine days. On the first six days, following the instructions for the appropriate verses, devote one prayer period to imaginatively contemplating each of the scriptural selections in the order you decided. On the seventh day, repeat the biblical verse that was most meaningful to you. On the eighth day, pick one verse at random (other than the one used on the 7th day) and contemplate it imaginatively. Finally, on the ninth day, incorporate all your experiences from the previous eight days in an application of the senses.

After completing the sequence of imaginative contemplations, review your notes for the entire subsection and mark those that are most significant or meaningful to you before proceeding to the next section. Ask God to continue supporting and sustaining your efforts to incorporate the virtue of each subsection into your life.

<u>Using the prayer sequences in each subsection:</u>

The prayer sequences (included as morning and evening prayers) in each subsection are meant to complement the reflections and imaginative contemplations in their respective subsection and they should be prayed every day you are engaged in the subsection. So, it is important that you decide how you will use these sequences while you are engaged in the subsection.

Your first decision relates to when you want to pray with these sequences. It is advisable that you pray the sequence is in a manner that balances your other prayers and reflections. For example, if you spend most of your time praying or reflecting in the morning, then you might find it best to pray the sequences in the evening (and vice versa). However, you may also decide to incorporate your imaginative contemplation into the sequence by substituting the reflection section following the gospel reading with your imaginative contemplation.

Your second decision involves the use of the biblical verses to be used in the sequences. There is no correlation between the individual biblical verses presented for imaginative contemplation except for their shared relationship to the themes of the subsection, so you may include them randomly in the prayer sequences. However, once you begin the imaginative contemplations, it is important that the scripture verse you are contemplating be included in your prayer with the sequences.

Finally, your third decision concerns whether you choose to pray alone or with others. If you choose to pray the sequences alone, then You make the previous decisions on your own and praise the sequences as outlined in each section. However, if you choose to pray with others, you will need to decide when (and where) you will pray the sequences. Also, if you use the sequences in a group, they should be read antiphonally with a leader or part of the group reading the lines on the margin and the rest of the group reading the indented lines. Also, it would be useful to decide beforehand who will read the gospel verse (and if this should change) and whether the group will read the psalm antiphonally or at the same time.

As you proceed through the following section, it is important that you remember that this is your experience and you should allow it to be shaped by your needs and capabilities. Still, it is important that you commit yourself completely to this process in a manner that offers you the most benefit – even if it is challenging. So, as you make your decisions about how to best proceed, you might find it helpful to review your retreat experiences and strive to follow the patterns of prayer (e.g., the times when you pray, the length of your prayer periods, etc.) that worked best for you during your retreat.

The exercises of this section expand on your retreat experiences during "(II) The Brothers Visit Holy Enda & An Uninhabited House" and "(III) The Island of Sheep & The Leviathan Jasconius" in A Pilgrimage to the Land of the Saints. Before proceeding to the following reflections and prayers, it might be helpful to review "Finding Christ in All Things" and "Sharing in the Love of the Trinity" following "(II) The Brothers Visit Holy Enda & An Uninhabited House" and "(III) The Island of Sheep & The Leviathan Jasconius" in the first section of A Journey to the Land of the Saints.

Faith cannot survive without purity of heart. It an act of love responding to a far greater love (see 1 John 4: 19), creating an asymmetrical relationship that requires you to humbly open yourself to God's love knowing you will never be able to fully reciprocate the gifts you receive from God. Humility of spirit and purity of heart allow you to embrace this imbalance and accept God's love with gratitude, rather than allow your pride and self-importance to subvert your relationship with God.

With this in mind, read this story of Ita's early life from Edward C. Sellner's *Wisdom of the Celtic Saints*:

Ita's Desire to be Consecrated to Christ, and Her Parents' Resistance

Ita came to her mother and announced to her the divine precepts the Holy Spirit had taught her. She asked her mother to seek her father's permission so that she might consecrate herself to Christ. But her father was defiantly opposed to what she desired. The request was also very displeasing to her mother, and when others added their petitions, Ita's father vehemently refused to give permission. Then Ita, filled with the spirit of prophecy, said to all: "Leave my father alone for a while. Though he now forbids me to be consecrated to Christ, he will come to persuade me and eventually will order me to do so, for he will be compelled by Jesus Christ my Lord to let me go wherever I wish to serve God." And it happened as she had predicted. This is how it came about.

20

Not long afterward, Ita fasted for three days and three nights. During those days and nights, through dreams and vigils, it became clear that the devil was waging several battles against Ita. She, however, resisted him in everything, whether she slept or watched. One night the devil, sad and grieving, left Ita with these words: "Alas, Ita, you will free yourself from me, and many others too will be delivered." That very night an angel of the Lord came to Ita's father and said: "Why do you forbid your daughter to accept the veil of virginity in Christ's name? For she will be a great and famous virgin before God and his saints and will be the protector of many on the Day of Judgment. You will not only allow her to accept the sign of virginity, but you will let her go wherever she wants in order to serve Christ. She will serve God in another people, and she will be the mother of that people." Hearing this, Ita's father came to her immediately and told her all that he had heard. As the virgin had foretold, he gave her his permission to leave, and also urged her to take the veil of virginity and to go wherever she wished. That very day, having completed the three-day fast, Ita went to the church to receive the veil.

Again, in a reflective manner, take time to prayerfully consider these questions and record your observations in your journal:

1.   Are you able to sustain the same faith as Ita? Does Ita's persistent belief that Jesus would guide her father to accept her vocation to become a nun encourage you?… Why? Does it challenge your lapses in faith? If so, what are the impediments you face in trusting so completely in God?

2.   Compare Ita with Brendan and his companions. Which qualities of faith do they share?… And which are different? What do these different ancient Celtic saints teach you about faith as a gift from God?… And as a disposition or habit learned from your experience of God?

3.   What does this story say to you about the God's presence in the world?… And in your life? What are the signs of that presence that you can rely upon as you strive to be faithful to God? How does God speak to Ita?… To her father?… To you?

4.   Do you hear God calling to you to some form of service?... What are you being asked to do? What are the challenges you face in answering that call?... From within yourself?... From other people in your life?... From the society in which you live?

If a particular question seems especially significant, give yourself the opportunity to linger on it and bring the concerns it arouses to your subsequent prayer.

Using the imaginative techniques employed during your retreat, contemplate on separate days the following scriptural verses:

Psalm 24
Psalm 62
Matthew 6: 25-34
Matthew 8: 5-13
Matthew 5: 1-11
2 Timothy 2: 20-25

Note: If you are praying in a place other than where you made your initial retreat, or if you are uncertain about where and when to pray, you might find it helpful to review the suggestions presented in "Building a Vessel for your Pilgrimage" in A Pilgrimage to the Land of the Saints.

In your imaginative contemplation of the psalms and the epistle, imagine Ita first praying and then teaching with others (making certain to note the place in which these events take place and the demeanor of Ita in these moments). Then, after you allow this scene to fade from your prayer, speak to Jesus about your observations and concerns as you did during your retreat. As always, remember to give space for Jesus to reply.

When praying with the Gospels, observe the place in which these events take place and the demeanor of Jesus in these moments. Then, after you allow this scene to fade from your prayer, speak to Jesus about your observations and concerns as you. Again, remember to give space for Jesus to reply.

My God, my God, Lord, I entreat you

a morning prayer

[Sources: *The Book of Cerne* (9th Century), *The Antiphonary of Bangor* (7th Century), and the Lorica of St. Fursey, (7th Century).]

My God, my God, Lord, I entreat you,
protect me so that I may love you.
    Instruct me, O Jesus, great Lamb of God.
You endeavored to save me.
    True God, have mercy, help, and preserve me.
King of saints and angels,
    protect me. Love me.
I believe in you, true God,
the same now as before,
    without end, holy Trinity,
    one God, yet not alone.
A threefold unity.
I appeal to your merit,
    do not charge us for our sins,
    but overlook them, erase them.

All:
Avert all threats from us,
so that the flaming arrows of the devil may be extinguished,
so that I may be sound now and in the future. Amen.

A Psalm or Epistolatory Selection, read or recited

O Lord, you are the light in the darkness,
    Creator of all the elements,
    Forgiver of our sins.
O Lord, may your great mercy be on us
    as we seek you with our whole heart.
We hear of your majesty, O Lord, in the morning.
    Blot out our sins, for nothing is hidden from you;

All:

who lives and reigns, one God, now and forever. Amen.

A Gospel Reading, read aloud or quietly

Reflection

> *Pause for a moment. Then, allow the images from your contemplation to rise in your memory. Permit each moment to congeal for a moment in your mind before receding into the narrative of the scripture verse.*
> *Afterward, after the images have passed from your consciousness, allow a single phrase from the reading to rise from the silence.*
> *Then, if alone, allow Jesus to sit with you in your imagination and briefly discuss the phrase reading with Him; if praying with others, discuss the reading with them.*
> *When you are ready, continue by praying:*

May the guiding hands of God be on my shoulders,
    may the presence of the Holy Spirit be on my head,
may the sign of Christ be on my forehead,
    may the voice of the Holy Spirit be in my ears,
may the smell of the Holy Spirit be in my nose,
    may the sight of the company of heaven be in my eyes,
may the speech of the company of heaven be in my mouth,
    may the work of the church of God be in my hands,
may the serving of God and my neighbor be in my feet,
    may God make my heart his home,

All:
and may I belong to God, my Father, completely.

Select one of the following options for the Lord's Prayer.

Option A

> "Our Father in heaven,
> hallowed be your name.
> Your kingdom come.
> Your will be done,

on earth as it is in heaven.
Give us this day our daily bread.
And forgive us our debts,
as we also have forgiven our debtors.
And do not bring us to the time of trial,
but rescue us from the evil one."
(Matthew 6: 9-13)

Proceed with "My God, my God, Lord, I entreat you...," found after
Option B

Option B

Our Father in heaven,
hallowed be your name,
your kingdom come,
your will be done,
on earth as in heaven.
Give us today our daily bread.
Forgive us our sins
as we forgive those who sin against us.
Lead us not into temptation
but deliver us from evil.

My God, my God, Lord, I entreat you,
protect me so that I may love you.
Instruct me, O Jesus, great Lamb of God.
You endeavored to save me.
True God, have mercy, help, and preserve me.
King of saints and angels,
protect me. Love me.
I believe in you, true God,
the same now as before,
without end, holy Trinity,
one God, yet not alone.
A threefold unity.
I appeal to your merit,
do not charge us for our sins,
but overlook them, erase them.

All:
Avert all threats from us,
so that the flaming arrows of the devil may be extinguished,
so that I may be sound now and in the future. Amen.

Immortal God, guardian over all

an evening prayer

[Sources: *The Book of Cerne* (9th Century), a 5th Century evensong attributed to Saint Patrick, and the Lorica of St. Fursey (7th Century).]

Immortal God,
guardian over all,
        give freedom to those who pray,
peace to those who ask,
        life to those who believe,
resurrection to the dead,
        hope to the faithful,
glorification to the humble,
        blessedness to the righteous
        who keep your commandments
in most holy love.
Grant these things to us,

All:
so that those who have been hurt by many things
may find your charity abounding in us;
through him who has cleansed all sins.

A Psalm or Epistolatory Selection, read or recited

May your holy angels, O Christ, Son of living God,
guard our sleep, our rest, our shining bed.
        Let them reveal true visions to us in our sleep,
O high Prince of the universe, O great King of the mysteries!
        May no demons, no ill, no calamity or terrifying dreams
        disturb our rest, our willing, prompt repose.

All:
May our watch be holy, our work, our task,
our sleep, our rest without let, without break.

A Gospel Reading, read aloud or quietly

Reflection

Pause for a moment. Then, allow the images from your contemplation to rise in your memory. Permit each moment to congeal for a moment in your mind before receding into the narrative of the scripture verse.

Afterward, after the images have passed from your consciousness, allow a single phrase from the reading to rise from the silence.

Then, if alone, allow Jesus to sit with you in your imagination and briefly discuss the phrase reading with Him; if praying with others, discuss the reading with them.

When you are ready, continue by praying:

May the guiding hands of God be on my shoulders,
    may the presence of the Holy Spirit be on my head,
may the sign of Christ be on my forehead,
    may the voice of the Holy Spirit be in my ears,
may the smell of the Holy Spirit be in my nose,
    may the sight of the company of heaven be in my eyes,
may the speech of the company of heaven be in my mouth,
    may the work of the church of God be in my hands,
may the serving of God and my neighbor be in my feet,
    may God make my heart his home,

All:
and may I belong to God, my Father, completely.

Select one of the following options for the Lord's Prayer.

Option A

"Our Father in heaven,
hallowed be your name.
Your kingdom come.
Your will be done,
on earth as it is in heaven.
Give us this day our daily bread.
And forgive us our debts,

as we also have forgiven our debtors.
And do not bring us to the time of trial,
but rescue us from the evil one."
(Matthew 6: 9-13)

*Proceed with "Immortal God, guardian over all...," found after
Option B*

Option B

Our Father in heaven,
hallowed be your name,
your kingdom come,
your will be done,
on earth as in heaven.
Give us today our daily bread.
Forgive us our sins
as we forgive those who sin against us.
Lead us not into temptation
but deliver us from evil.

Immortal God,
guardian over all,
give freedom to those who pray,
peace to those who ask,
life to those who believe,
resurrection to the dead,
hope to the faithful,
glorification to the humble,
blessedness to the righteous
who keep your commandments
in most holy love.
Grant these things to us,

All:
so that those who have been hurt by many things
may find your charity abounding in us;
through him who has cleansed all sins. Amen.

'A Simple Life with a Grateful Spirit'

The exercises of this section expand on your retreat experiences during "(V) The Community of Ailbe" in A Pilgrimage to the Land of the Saints. *Before proceeding to the following reflections and prayers, it might be helpful to review "Living as Citizens of Heaven" following "(V) The Community of Ailbe" in the first section of* A Journey to the Land of the Saints.

Living simply makes you aware of the many gifts that you receive from God each day, both large and small. It deepens and extends your feelings of gratitude while reminding you of the subtle temptations of inordinate materialism. Limiting your material possessions to only what you need strengthens your relationship with God heightens your awareness of the sinful temptations around you.

With this in mind, read this of Ita selecting the home of her community story from Edward C. Sellner's *Wisdom of the Celtic Saints*:

Ita Finds a Place for Her Monastery

As Ita was journeying, a great crowd of demons approached her and began to attack her fiercely. The angels of God descended from the heavens and fought strongly with the demons on Ita's behalf. Overcome by the angels the demons fled in all directions crying out and saying, "Woe to us, for from this day on we will not be able to fight against this virgin." In the meantime, Ita, consoled by the angels, came to a church where she was consecrated by the clerics at the angels' command and received the veil of virginity.

Then Ita prayed to the Lord to show her the place where she should serve him. An angel of the Lord came to her and said: "Leave your native district and come to the area called Ui Conaill and remain in the western part of it, near the foot of Sliabh Luachra. There the angel of the Lord will come to you and will show you the place where your convent will be. You will be the patron of the people of Ui Conaill; God has granted that people to you and to St. Senan." When Ita heard

30

these words from the angel, she went with her companions to that region and remained at the foot of Sliabh Luachra, as the angel had told her. The angel came to her immediately and assigned her the place where she would serve God.

From there the fame of Ita travelled throughout the entire region. Many virgins came to her from different places to serve God under her care. She received them all piously and cheerfully. Having heard of her great holiness, the people of Ui Conaill came with their chieftain and wanted to donate all the land around her cell to her and to God in perpetuity. Ita, however, did not wish to be involved in worldly concerns, and she accepted only four acres as a vegetable garden. The chieftain and his followers were very displeased by that and they said, "What you do not wish to accept now, when you go to God's kingdom, will be bestowed upon you." And so it happened. All the people of Ui Conaill took Ita as their patron from then on, as the angel had foretold. Ita blessed that people and their land with many blessings. They all returned home with great joy, and it became their custom to bring many gifts and alms to the monastery in honor of St. Ita for the use of the holy virgins.

Consider each question separately and record your observations in your journal:

1.   Do you see any parallels between the demons attacking Ita before her consecration and the displeasure of the people when Ita would only except four acres of land for her community? How did each group tempt Ita as she sought simplicity in her life?

2.   What are the temptations you face in trying to live simply and in harmony with God's desires for you? Which of these temptations emerge from within you?... And which temptations confront you through the actions of others?... And of the society in which you live?

3.   What does this story say to you about the need for simplicity in your spiritual life?... And the need to listen to God as you make decisions about your own life?... And your relationship with others? What does the story say to you about your need to trust in God's providence?... And your need to be grateful for the gifts God provides to you?

31

4.   How does the establishment of her monastery reflect Ita's personal journey?… And her service to the people around her monastic community? How does your personal spiritual journey involve others?… Your family and friends?… Strangers?

Again, linger on any questions that seem especially significant and bring these concerns to your subsequent prayer.

Using the imaginative techniques employed during your retreat, contemplate on separate days the following scriptural verses:
Psalm 103
Psalm 138
Luke 14: 7-11
Luke 17: 11-19
John 9: 1-11
Colossians 3: 3-17

Again, in your imaginative contemplation of the psalms and the epistle, imagine Ita praying and then teaching with others. Then, after you allow this scene to fade from your prayer, speak to Jesus about your observations and concerns as you did during your retreat. As always, remember to give space for Jesus to reply.

When praying with the Gospels, observe the place in which these events take place and the demeanor of Jesus in these moments. Then, speak to Jesus about your observations and concerns as you. Remember to give space for Jesus to reply.

Let angels, hosts and powers praise you

a morning prayer

[Sources: *The Antiphonary of Bangor* (7th Century) and the Lorica of St. Fursey, (7th Century).]

Let angels, hosts, stars, powers
and whatever proceeds from them
praise you, O Lord.
> Let them give service and exult in your praise,
> that harmony may be sung to you
> throughout the universe,
and that your will may be done
> in heaven and on earth.
Let your favor be upon your people, we pray,
> O Lord, that by exalting you with our joined voices,
> we may remain as one,
armed with your Word which you speak,
> and our lives always contemplating your truth and salvation,
> which you have shown in your surpassing greatness.
We praise you, O Lord.
> We display our praise with thanks.
We praise you with lute and harp,
> with tambourine and dance,
with strings and pipe,
> with sounding cymbals,

All:
that we may always receive your mercy,
O Christ, Savior of the world;
with the eternal Father you live and reign
with the eternal Holy Spirit,
forever and ever. Amen.

A Psalm or Epistolatory Selection, read or recited

O Lord,
hear us as we pray to you

in the beginning hours of this day.
>We give you thanks,
>O Lord our God,
>for you have redeemed us with your holy blood
and you give your kind help
>in answer to the early prayers and petitions we bring you;
you reign with the Father and the Holy Spirit,
>one God, now and forever. Amen.

A Gospel Reading, read aloud or quietly

Reflection

Pause for a moment. Then, allow the images from your contemplation to rise in your memory. Permit each moment to congeal for a moment in your mind before receding into the narrative of the scripture verse.

Afterward, after the images have passed from your consciousness, allow a single phrase from the reading to rise from the silence.

Then, if alone, allow Jesus to sit with you in your imagination and briefly discuss the phrase reading with Him; if praying with others, discuss the reading with them.

When you are ready, continue by praying:

May the guiding hands of God be on my shoulders,
>may the presence of the Holy Spirit be on my head,
may the sign of Christ be on my forehead,
>may the voice of the Holy Spirit be in my ears,
may the smell of the Holy Spirit be in my nose,
>may the sight of the company of heaven be in my eyes,
may the speech of the company of heaven be in my mouth,
>may the work of the church of God be in my hands,
may the serving of God and my neighbor be in my feet,
>may God make my heart his home,

All:
and may I belong to God, my Father, completely.

Select one of the following options for the Lord's Prayer.

Option A

> "Our Father in heaven,
> hallowed be your name.
> Your kingdom come.
> Your will be done,
> on earth as it is in heaven.
> Give us this day our daily bread.
> And forgive us our debts,
> as we also have forgiven our debtors.
> And do not bring us to the time of trial,
> but rescue us from the evil one."
> (Matthew 6: 9-13)

Proceed with "Let angels, hosts, stars, powers…," found after Option B

Option B

> Our Father in heaven,
> hallowed be your name,
> your kingdom come,
> your will be done,
> on earth as in heaven.
> Give us today our daily bread.
> Forgive us our sins
> as we forgive those who sin against us.
> Lead us not into temptation
> but deliver us from evil.

Let angels, hosts, stars, powers
and whatever proceeds from them
praise you, O Lord.
> Let them give service and exult in your praise,
> that harmony may be sung to you
> throughout the universe,
and that your will may be done
> in heaven and on earth.
Let your favor be upon your people, we pray,

O Lord, that by exalting you with our joined voices,
   we may remain as one,
armed with your Word which you speak,
   and our lives always contemplating your truth and salvation,
   which you have shown in your surpassing greatness.
We praise you, O Lord.
   We display our praise with thanks.
We praise you with lute and harp,
   with tambourine and dance,
with strings and pipe,
   with sounding cymbals,

All:
that we may always receive your mercy,
O Christ, Savior of the world;
with the eternal Father you live and reign
with the eternal Holy Spirit,
forever and ever. Amen.

Lord, open your heavens, open our eyes

an evening prayer

[Sources: *The Benedictionale of St. Ethelwold* (10th Century), *The Antiphonary of Bangor* (7th Century), and the Lorica of St. Fursey, (7th Century).]

Lord, open your heavens, open our eyes.
From there your gifts descend to us,
from here may our hearts look back to you.
        May your throne be open to us
        as we receive the benefits we ask.
May our minds be open to you
while we serve as you have commanded us.
        Look down from heaven, O Lord.
        Visit and tend this vine you have planted.
Strengthen the weak,
        relieve the contrite,
confirm the strong.
        Build them up in love,
cleanse them with purity,
        enlighten them with wisdom,
keep them with mercy.
        Lord Jesus, Good Shepherd,
you laid down your life for the sheep.
        Defend those you purchased with your blood.
Feed the hungry,
        give drink to the thirsty,
seek the lost,
        call back the wandering,
heal what is broken.
        Stretch forth your hand from heaven
and touch the head of each one.

All:
May they feel the touch of your hand
and receive the joy of the Holy Spirit,
that they may remain blessed forevermore.

A Psalm or Epistolatory Selection, read or recited

As the time of day is turning
and the night is coming over us,
> let us pray for the mercy of God,
> that we may increase in our divine knowledge
and renounce the works of darkness;
> you reign as one God, now and forever.

A Gospel Reading, read aloud or quietly

Reflection

> *Pause for a moment. Then, allow the images from your contemplation to rise in your memory. Permit each moment to congeal for a moment in your mind before receding into the narrative of the scripture verse.*
> *Afterward, after the images have passed from your consciousness, allow a single phrase from the reading to rise from the silence.*
> *Then, if alone, allow Jesus to sit with you in your imagination and briefly discuss the phrase reading with Him; if praying with others, discuss the reading with them.*
> *When you are ready, continue by praying:*

May the guiding hands of God be on my shoulders,
> may the presence of the Holy Spirit be on my head,
may the sign of Christ be on my forehead,
> may the voice of the Holy Spirit be in my ears,
may the smell of the Holy Spirit be in my nose,
> may the sight of the company of heaven be in my eyes,
may the speech of the company of heaven be in my mouth,
> may the work of the church of God be in my hands,
may the serving of God and my neighbor be in my feet,
> may God make my heart his home,

All:
and may I belong to God, my Father, completely.

Select one of the following options for the Lord's Prayer.

Option A

> "Our Father in heaven,
> hallowed be your name.
> Your kingdom come.
> Your will be done,
> on earth as it is in heaven.
> Give us this day our daily bread.
> And forgive us our debts,
> as we also have forgiven our debtors.
> And do not bring us to the time of trial,
> but rescue us from the evil one."
> (Matthew 6: 9-13)

Proceed with "Lord, open your heavens, open our eyes...," found after Option B

Option B

> Our Father in heaven,
> hallowed be your name,
> your kingdom come,
> your will be done,
> on earth as in heaven.
> Give us today our daily bread.
> Forgive us our sins
> as we forgive those who sin against us.
> Lead us not into temptation
> but deliver us from evil.

Lord, open your heavens, open our eyes.
From there your gifts descend to us,
from here may our hearts look back to you.
> May your throne be open to us
> as we receive the benefits we ask.
May our minds be open to you
while we serve as you have commanded us.
> Look down from heaven, O Lord.

Visit and tend this vine you have planted.
Strengthen the weak,
　　　relieve the contrite,
confirm the strong.
　　　Build them up in love,
cleanse them with purity,
　　　enlighten them with wisdom,
keep them with mercy.
　　　Lord Jesus, Good Shepherd,
you laid down your life for the sheep.
　　　Defend those you purchased with your blood.
Feed the hungry,
　　　give drink to the thirsty,
seek the lost,
　　　call back the wandering,
heal what is broken.
　　　Stretch forth your hand from heaven
and touch the head of each one.

All:
May they feel the touch of your hand
and receive the joy of the Holy Spirit,
that they may remain blessed forevermore.

The exercises of this section expand on your retreat experiences during "(VII) Unhappy Judas" and "(VIII) The Island of Paul the Hermit" in A Pilgrimage to the Land of the Saints. *Before proceeding to the following reflections and prayers, it might be helpful to review "Embracing the Standard of Christ" and "Welcoming Others into the Resurrection" following "(VII) Unhappy Judas" and "(VIII) The Island of Paul the Hermit" in the first section of* A Journey to the Land of the Saints.

The gifts you receive from God in love evoke generosity and compassion toward others. These gestures of love transform human interactions through acts of kindness and forgiveness, creating what the ancient Celtic saints called "colonies of heaven" here on earth.

With this in mind, read these two stories from Edward C. Sellner's *Wisdom of the Celtic Saints*:

Ita's Effectiveness as a Confessor

A nun who had been under Ita's charge committed fornication. On the following day, Ita summoned her and said: "Why did you not care, sister, to guard your virginity?" The nun, however, denied that she had committed fornication. Ita said to her: "Did you really not commit fornication yesterday in such-and-such a place?" The nun saw immediately that Ita could prophesy about things past and present. She admitted the truth and was healed, doing penance according to Ita's command.

Another virgin, living far away from Ita in the province of Connacht, secretly committed adultery. Full of the spirit of prophecy, Ita knew this, and ordered St. Brendan to bring the nun to her. St. Brendan made the woman go to Ita. Ita then described to her, among other things, how she had conceived and given birth to a son. When the woman heard her sin from Ita's mouth, she made a fitting penance. Her soul was restored to eternal salvation, and afterward she led a holy life.

Ita, the Confessor, Keeps Her Promise

A certain man killed his brother. Touched with remorse, he came to Ita and did penance according to her command. Ita, seeing his devout heart, said: "If you obey my words, you will not have a sudden death, but you will go to eternal life." It happened afterward that he went with his chieftain to fight, for he was a soldier, and the battle went against them, and he was killed. When Ita heard that, she said: "I promised that man that he would have a happy end to his life because he listened to my advice." She said to her attendants: "Go, find him in the devastation, and call upon him in God's name and mine. I believe he will rise and meet you." They did as she said, and the dead man rose from the battle as if he had never been killed. He ran toward those who were searching for him and came with them to Ita. Afterward everything turned out as Ita had promised.

Consider these questions and record your observations in your journal:

1.   How does Ita's response to the nuns' sinfulness reflect her awareness both of the power of God's forgiveness and of the continuing presence of sin in the world? How does her response help you understand God's love of you and forgiveness of your sins?

2.   Have you ever experienced God's complete forgiveness of your sins while knowing you remain a sinner? If so, how has this experience changed you?… Changed your relationships with others?… Changed your relationship with God? If not, what do you think are the impediments to your sins being forgiven?

3.   How does the story of a man being brought back to life help you better understand the meaning of Jesus' resurrection?… In your own life?… And for the world? Why is it important to have a relationship with the risen Christ?… And why is it important to share this relationship with others?

4.   How might you share your experiences of God's love and forgiveness?

42

Remember to linger on a particular questions that seem especially significant and bring these concerns to your subsequent prayer.

Using the imaginative techniques employed during your retreat, contemplate on separate days the following scriptural verses:

Psalm 32
Matthew 20: 1-16
Luke 6: 20-36
John 15: 1-17
1 Corinthians 13: 1-13
2 Corinthians 8: 8-15

Again, in your imaginative contemplation of the psalms and the epistle, imagine Ita praying and then teaching with others before speaking to Jesus about your observations and concerns as you did during your retreat.

When praying with the Gospels, observe the place in which these events take place and the demeanor of Jesus in these moments before speaking to about your observations and concerns as you. Remember to give space for Jesus to reply.

The will of God be done by us

a morning prayer

[Sources: *The Religious Songs of Connacht* (1906), *The Antiphonary of Bangor* (7th Century), and the Lorica of St. Fursey, (7th Century).]

The will of God be done by us,
    the law of God be kept by us,
our evil will controlled by us,
    our tongue in check be held by us,
repentance timely made by us,
    Christ's passion understood by us,
each sinful crime be shunned by us,
    much on the end be mused by us,
and blessed death be found by us,
    with angels' music heard by us,

All:
and God's high praises sung to us,
forever and for aye. Amen.

A Psalm or Epistolatory Selection, read or recited

O Lord, you are the light in the darkness,
Creator of all the elements,
Forgiver of our sins.
    O Lord, may your great mercy be on us
    as we seek you with our whole heart.
We hear of your majesty, O Lord, in the morning.
    Blot out our sins, for nothing is hidden from you;

All:
who lives and reigns, one God, now and forever. Amen.

A Gospel Reading, read aloud or quietly

Reflection

Pause for a moment. Then, allow the images from your contemplation to rise in your memory. Permit each moment to congeal for a moment in your mind before receding into the narrative of the scripture verse.

Afterward, after the images have passed from your consciousness, allow a single phrase from the reading to rise from the silence.

Then, if alone, allow Jesus to sit with you in your imagination and briefly discuss the phrase reading with Him; if praying with others, discuss the reading with them.

When you are ready, continue by praying:

May the guiding hands of God be on my shoulders,
    may the presence of the Holy Spirit be on my head,
may the sign of Christ be on my forehead,
    may the voice of the Holy Spirit be in my ears,
may the smell of the Holy Spirit be in my nose,
    may the sight of the company of heaven be in my eyes,
may the speech of the company of heaven be in my mouth,
    may the work of the church of God be in my hands,
may the serving of God and my neighbor be in my feet,
    may God make my heart his home,

All:
and may I belong to God, my Father, completely.

Select one of the following options for the Lord's Prayer.

Option A

    "Our Father in heaven,
    hallowed be your name.
    Your kingdom come.
    Your will be done,
    on earth as it is in heaven.
    Give us this day our daily bread.
    And forgive us our debts,
    as we also have forgiven our debtors.
    And do not bring us to the time of trial,
    but rescue us from the evil one."

(Matthew 6: 9-13)

Proceed with "The will of God be done by us...," found after Option B

Option B

>Our Father in heaven,
>hallowed be your name,
>your kingdom come,
>your will be done,
>on earth as in heaven.
>Give us today our daily bread.
>Forgive us our sins
>as we forgive those who sin against us.
>Lead us not into temptation
>but deliver us from evil.

The will of God be done by us,
> the law of God be kept by us,
our evil will controlled by us,
> our tongue in check be held by us,
repentance timely made by us,
> Christ's passion understood by us,
each sinful crime be shunned by us,
> much on the end be mused by us,
and blessed death be found by us,
> with angels' music heard by us,

All:
and God's high praises sung to us,
forever and for aye. Amen.

Life be in my speech, sense in what I say

an evening prayer

[Sources: An anonymous Irish poem (12th Century or later), Gaelic prayer (possibly used by Columban monks), a 5th Century evensong attributed to Saint Patrick, and the Lorica of St. Fursey (7th Century).]

Life be in my speech,
> sense in what I say,
the bloom of cherries on my lips,
> till I come back again.
The love Jesus Christ gave
> be filling every heart for me,
the love Jesus Christ gave
> filling me for everyone.
Traversing corries traversing forests,
> traversing valleys long and wild,

All:
the Shepherd Jesus still uphold me,
the Shepherd Jesus be my shield.

A Psalm or Epistolatory Selection, read or recited

May your holy angels, O Christ, Son of living God,
guard our sleep, our rest, our shining bed.
> Let them reveal true visions to us in our sleep,
> O high Prince of the universe, O great King of the mysteries!
May no demons, no ill, no calamity or terrifying dreams
disturb our rest, our willing, prompt repose.
> May our watch be holy, our work, our task,
> our sleep, our rest without let, without break.

A Gospel Reading, read aloud or quietly

Reflection

Pause for a moment. Then, allow the images from your contemplation to rise in your memory. Permit each moment to congeal for a moment in your mind before receding into the narrative of the scripture verse.

Afterward, after the images have passed from your consciousness, allow a single phrase from the reading to rise from the silence.

Then, if alone, allow Jesus to sit with you in your imagination and briefly discuss the phrase reading with Him; if praying with others, discuss the reading with them.

When you are ready, continue by praying:

May the guiding hands of God be on my shoulders,
    may the presence of the Holy Spirit be on my head,
may the sign of Christ be on my forehead,
    may the voice of the Holy Spirit be in my ears,
may the smell of the Holy Spirit be in my nose,
    may the sight of the company of heaven be in my eyes,
may the speech of the company of heaven be in my mouth,
    may the work of the church of God be in my hands,
may the serving of God and my neighbor be in my feet,
    may God make my heart his home,

All:
and may I belong to God, my Father, completely.

Select one of the following options for the Lord's Prayer.

Option A

> "Our Father in heaven,
> hallowed be your name.
> Your kingdom come.
> Your will be done,
> on earth as it is in heaven.
> Give us this day our daily bread.
> And forgive us our debts,
> as we also have forgiven our debtors.
> And do not bring us to the time of trial,
> but rescue us from the evil one."

(Matthew 6: 9-13)

Proceed with "Life be in my speech...," found after Option B

Option B

> Our Father in heaven,
> hallowed be your name,
> your kingdom come,
> your will be done,
> on earth as in heaven.
> Give us today our daily bread.
> Forgive us our sins
> as we forgive those who sin against us.
> Lead us not into temptation
> but deliver us from evil.

Life be in my speech,
      sense in what I say,
the bloom of cherries on my lips,
      till I come back again.
The love Jesus Christ gave
      be filling every heart for me,
the love Jesus Christ gave
      filling me for everyone.
Traversing corries traversing forests,
      traversing valleys long and wild,

All:
the Shepherd Jesus still uphold me,
the Shepherd Jesus be my shield.

Creating Enclaves of Hope

Considerations

For the ancient Celtic saints, spirituality was not a private matter. They saw themselves as "colonies of heaven" living here on earth. For them, the obligations of this sacred citizenship required them to act towards everyone with justice and mercy – and to share with others the joy of living in a redeemed world. With this in mind, the prayers and exercises of this section are designed to help you live as "citizens of heaven" – making social and cultural choices in your day-to-day life based on the ideals of the gospel – and testify to the possibilities of living the gospel while building the Kingdom of God here on earth.

Before approaching each subsection:

As in the previous sections, you should review your retreat journal to see if there are any significant periods of prayer during the days/weeks addressed in each of the following subsections. If so, take your time enjoying the memories of your retreat experience and the particular graces or insights from your earlier prayers. If you repeated any of these prayers during the interval between your retreat and now, consider these repetitions and note any differences between these two (or more) experiences with regard to content or emotional energy. Afterward, write your observations in your journal.

Also, reread the reflections for the relevant days/weeks in the first section of *A Journey to the Land of the Saints*. Consider your initial answers the review questions and exercises at the end of these readings, reflecting on how these answers may have changed during the months since you first approached them. If you did not complete these review questions and exercises earlier, take time to consider them now in a contemplative manner. Again, write your observations in your journal.

Approaching "Sacred Citizenship & the Challenge of Hope"

When you are ready, begin by reading the story about Canair at the beginning of the subsection and answering the questions that follow it.

Begin by reading the story slowly and contemplatively, discerning any connections you feel between it and the prayers of your retreat. Then reflectively the questions following the story, deciding if there are any questions you might want to answer together. Finally, record in your journal any insights or observations you might have about the story as well as any graces you might request as you consider the interaction between Canair and Senan.

Then, on separate days, address each question (or cluster of questions). Begin by asking God's help in understanding Canair's desires and Senan's response to them. Reread the question slowly, noting any significant phrases or words in it before answering the question and recording it in your journal. As in the previous section, it is important that you take as much time as you want (or feel you need) in answering each question, even if this means extending the process and spending more than one day on a particular issue or concern.

Note: Again, as with your reflections on the readings in the previous sections, you might find it helpful to imagine yourself answering the question in the presence of Jesus, speaking with him about the nuances of the question(s) and your responses to them.

After completing your consideration of the questions, devote a prayer session to prayerfully reviewing your answers. Ask God to reveal the graces you will need to ask for in the imaginative contemplations. Then, as in the previous section, read the scriptural verses presented for contemplation and decide the order in which you would like to contemplate them -- beginning with the biblical verse that seems most relevant to your current situation. If you do not feel led to organize the biblical verses in a particular manner, place them in a random order before beginning your contemplations.

Approach the biblical verses over the course of six days. On the first four days, imaginatively contemplate each of the scriptural selections in the order you decided. On the fifth day, repeat the biblical verse that was most meaningful to you. Finally, on the sixth day, incorporate all your experiences from the previous six days in an application of the senses.

As you did in the previous section, review your notes and mark those that are most significant or meaningful to you before proceeding to the following exercises. Ask God to continue supporting and sustaining your prayers and reflections before proceeding to the reflection exercises.

> Note: It is important that you proceed through the reflection exercises in order since they build upon one another.

As you begin "Circles of Compassion & Action", take time to review the instructions. Again, the amount of time you spend on these reflections each day should be the same that which you allocate for your prayer periods. So, as you look at the various levels, you may decide to work on more than one during a given day but, if you make this choice, it is important that the levels are connected to one another and do not have another level separating them (e.g., Levels A & B may be clustered together but Levels A & C cannot, Level C & D may be clustered together but not Levels C & E, etc.).

> Note: Take as many or as few days as you need to complete this exercise but make certain that you have devoted as much time and energy to this as you need to properly complete the exercise.

After completing "Circles of Compassion & Action", devote at least six days to the exercises in "Laments, Litanies and Loricas". During your imaginative contemplations of the laments and litanies, make certain that you allow time for the sentiments of your prayer to fully settle into your consciousness. Pay attention to the rhythms of the prayer and the emotional shifts within it, being careful to include these observations in your journal after your prayers. Then, when asked to write your own lament or litany, make certain to incorporate these dynamics into your own prayers.

> Note: When writing your own lament or litany (or the "defense statements" of the lorica), do not be afraid to "overwrite". Make certain it is a complete statement of your personal needs or the needs of others.

Finally, you will need to decide which of the prayers in "Laments, Litanies and Loricas" should remain private and which you want to share with others. Remember, while our spiritual lives should never remain entirely private, our deepest prayers also reveal our weaknesses and insecurities as we brief them before God. So, as you compose these prayers, remain aware that you may wish to write them in two formats: a first that intimately expresses your neediness before God while another is meant to be a public statement of companionship.

Approaching "Articulate Witness & the Virtue of Hospitality"

Unlike the decision about sharing or not sharing your prayers in "Laments, Litanies and Loricas", the exercises in this subsection are intended to guide you towards a deliberate public statement of faith based on your intimate relationship with God. In these exercises, there is greater emphasis placed on style and expression than on content – although all three are very important to the act of witness at the heart of the exercises. For this reason, you should allow yourself as much time as you need to polish your creative work as you move from sharing it with or select (and receptive) audience before introducing it to strangers.

With these considerations in mind, it might be useful to use a separate notebook while developing the creative work emerging from the exercises in this subsection. While there are certain aspects of the exercises specifically intended to be recorded in your retreat Journal, these are meant to delineate the connective tissue between your prayer and your creative expression. The various versions or drafts of your creative work will evolve over time until you feel they "complete" and you are comfortable with sharing them with others. If you are truly honest with yourself, and do not allow your insecurities to impede your judgment, you will know when this moment has arrived.

The exercises of this section expand on your retreat experiences during "(VI) The Crystal Pillar & The Island of Smiths" in A Pilgrimage to the Land of the Saints. *Before proceeding to the following reflections and prayers, it might be helpful to review "Learning the Patterns of God's Presence" following "(VI) The Crystal Pillar & The Island of Smiths" in the first section of* A Journey to the Land of the Saints.

As a "citizen of heaven", you are commissioned to manifest God's love in a world mired in anger, distrust and hatred. Your calling to live as a child of God requires you to cultivate hope amidst despair. It asks that you express the possibilities of a new world in the face of complacent acceptance of "the world as it is". Becoming a "living sign" of God's presence in the world involves recognizing that even your smallest actions in the face of pessimism and despair foster hope and optimism in others.

With this in mind, consider this story of Canair and Senan from Edward C. Sellner's *Wisdom of the Celtic Saints* (which is sometimes attributed to Senan and his missionary step-sister, Conainne).

Note: You may recall that Senan is mentioned in the story of Ita finding a place for her monastery. Ita and Senan were contemporaries (with Ita being slightly older but surviving Senan by 26 years) and were spiritual co-patrons of the area of southern Ireland where they both lived.

Canair's Persistence

Canair the Pious, a holy woman living in the south of Ireland, set up a hermitage in her own territory. One night, while she was praying, all the churches of Ireland appeared to her in a vision. It seemed as if a tower of fire rose up to heaven from each of the churches. The highest of the towers of fire, and the straightest toward heaven, was that which rose from Inis Cathaig (Scattery Island). "Fair is Senan's cell," Canair said. "I will go there, that my resurrection may be near it." She went immediately, without guidance except for the tower of fire, which she saw continuing to blaze day and night until she arrived. Now, when she had reached the shore, she walked upon the sea as if she were on smooth land until she came to Inis Cathaig. Senan knew that she was coming, and he went to the harbor to meet and welcome her.

"Yes, I have come," Canair told him.

"Go to your sister who lives on the island to the east of this one, so that you may be her guest," said Senan.

"That is not why I came," said Canair, "but that I may find hospitality with you on this island."

"Women cannot enter on this island," Senan replied.

"How can you say that?" asked Canair. "Christ is no worse than you. Christ came to redeem women no less than to redeem men. He suffered for the sake of women as much as for the sake of men. Women as well as men can enter the heavenly kingdom. Why, then, should you not allow women to live on this island?"

"You are persistent," said Senan.

"Well then," Canair replied, "will I get what I ask for? Will you give me a place to live on this island and the holy sacrament of eucharist?"

"Yes, Canair, a place of resurrection will be given you here on the brink of the waves," said Senan. She came on shore then, received the sacrament from Senan, and immediately went to heaven.

Again, consider these questions and record your observations in your journal:

1.   How do you see Canair and Senan? Is Canair promoting justice for women?… Or asserting her own entitlement? Is Senan protecting his principles?… Or demonstrating his misogyny? Perhaps you see them in entirely different ways. If so, how?

2.   Both Canair and Senan were regarded as saints by the ancient Celtic Christians. How do each of them convey their sanctity? How do each convey their humanity? Which aspects of their behavior inspire you?... And which disturb you?

3.   Are Canair and Senan engaged in a spiritual conversation searching for God's desires?... Or are they merely arguing? Which aspects of their conversation lead you to this conclusion?

4.   What does the conversation between Canair and Senan teach you about the nature of spiritual discernment? How does it help you to better recognize the patterns of God's loving activity in your life and in the world around you? How does it help you learn how to overcome your resistance to God's desires?

Remember to linger on any questions that seem especially significant and bring these concerns to your subsequent prayer.

Using the imaginative techniques employed during your retreat, contemplate on separate days the following scriptural verses:

Isaiah 61: 1-11
Luke 11: 5-13
Luke 18: 1-8
Galatians 6: 1-10

In your imaginative contemplation of Isaiah and the epistle, imagine Ita praying and then teaching with others before speaking to Jesus about your observations and concerns as you did during your retreat.

When praying with the Gospels, observe the place in which these events take place and the demeanor of Jesus in these moments before speaking to about your observations and concerns as you. Remember to give space for Jesus to reply.

In this exercise, consider the issues and problems that animate your social consciousness as well as your responses to them.

1.   On a large sheet of paper or whiteboard, draw six concentric circles and a line intersecting all six circles so that it cuts all of them in half. Finally, beginning with the inner-most circle, label each circle as "A" through "F". This should leave you with a diagram that looks something like this:

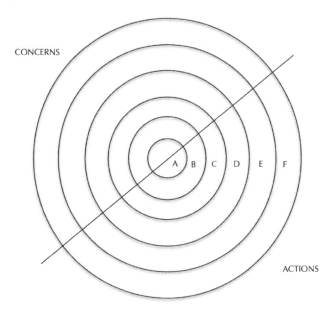

2.   Look at the inner-most circle (A). This circle represents you and your experiences.
        (a)   Ask... Have you faced any injustices or social inequities in your own life? Were you treated unfairly or coerced by others? Were you bullied in any way? Do you face discrimination or ostracism because of who you are? If so, mark an "x" on the "Concerns" half of the circle.
        (b)   At the top of a separate sheet of paper or notebook page, write "A - Self". Under this, list the issues or concerns you experience(d)

in your life. Leave ample space under each problem to write about the various responses to these personal injustices.

(c)   Under each issue, begin by listing examples of how you addressed this issue in your own life. In each case, distinguish between actions that mitigated or lessened the impact of this problem in your life from those that solved or eliminated the problem from your life.

(d)   Afterward, list examples of how other people challenged this issue in your life or defended you from its effects. Again, in each case, distinguish between actions that mitigated or lessened the impact of this problem in your life from those that solved or eliminated the problem from your life.

(e)   Finally, on a scale from 0 to 10 (with zero meaning there has been effective response to any of the issues and 10 indicated that all the issues have been eliminated), provide an assessment of the overall response(s) to each issue in terms of their effectiveness.

(f) Average the numbers associated all of the responses to all of the issues you have listed and place this number in the "Actions" side of the inner-most circle.

3.   Look at the second inner-most circle (B). This circle represents your family and its experiences.

(a)   Ask… Has your family faced any injustices or social inequities, directly or indirectly? Has your family been treated unfairly or felt coerced by others? Has your family experienced discrimination or ostracism because of who you are? If so, mark an "x" on the "Concerns" half of the circle.

(b)   Again, at the top of a separate sheet of paper or notebook page, write "B - Family". Under this, list the issues or concerns experienced by your family. Leave space under each problem to write about the various responses to these injustices.

(c)   Under each issue, begin by listing examples of how you addressed this issue on behalf of your family or you. In each case, distinguish between actions that mitigated or lessened the impact of this problem from those that solved or eliminated the problem from your life.

(d)   Afterward, list examples of how other people challenged this issue on behalf of your family or defended you or the members of your family from its effects. Again, distinguish in each case between actions that mitigated or lessened the impact of this problem for your family from those that solved or eliminated the problem.

(e)   Finally, on a scale from 0 to 10, provide an assessment of the overall response(s) to each issue in terms of their effectiveness.

(f) Average the numbers associated the responses to all of the issues you have listed and place this number in the "Actions" side of the second inner-most circle.

4.   Look at the third circle (C). This circle represents your friends and their experiences.

(a)   Ask... Have any of your friends faced any injustices or social inequities in their lives, directly or indirectly? Were they treated unfairly or coerced by others? Were they bullied in any way? Did they face discrimination or ostracism because of who they are? If so, mark an "x" on the "Concerns" half of the circle.

(b)   Write "C - Friends" at the top of a separate sheet of paper or notebook page. Under this, list the issues or concerns experienced by your friends. Leave space under each problem to write about the various responses to these injustices.

(c)   Under each issue, begin by listing examples of how you addressed this issue on behalf of your friends. Again, distinguish between actions that mitigated or lessened the impact of this problem from those that solved or eliminated the problem from your life.

(d)   Afterward, list examples of how other people challenged this issue on behalf of one or more of your friends or defended your friend(s) from its effects. Again, in each case, distinguish between actions that mitigated or lessened the impact of this problem for your friend(s) from those that solved or eliminated the problem.

(e)   Finally, on a scale from 0 to 10, provide an assessment of the overall response(s) to each issue in terms of their effectiveness.

(f) Average the numbers associated all of the responses to the issues you have listed and place this number in the "Actions" side of the third circle.

5.   Look at the fourth circle (D). This circle represents your local community and its experiences. This may involve people with whom you have a direct relationship, those with whom you have only a passing acquaintance, and those who you do not know personally.

(a)   Ask... Are there any social problems or injustices found in your local community? Are there health or environmental problems in your community? Are there people who face injustice or social inequity in their lives, directly or indirectly? Are there people who are treated unfairly or coerced by others? Are there examples of social and personal bullying? Do any members of your local community face discrimination or ostracism because of who they are? If so, mark an "x" on the "Concerns" half of the circle.

(b)   Write "D – Local Community" at the top of a separate sheet of paper or notebook page. Under this, list the social problems and injustices found in your local community. Again, leave space under each problem to write about the various responses to these concerns.

(c)   Under each issue, begin by listing examples of how you addressed this issue on behalf of your friends. Again, distinguish between actions that mitigated or lessened the impact of this problem from those that solved or eliminated the problem from your life.

(d)   Afterward, list examples of how other people in your community challenged this issue or protected your community from its effects. Again, in each case, distinguish between actions that mitigated or lessened the impact of this problem for your family from those that solved or eliminated the problem.

(e)   Finally, on a scale from 0 to 10, provide an assessment of the overall response(s) to each issue in terms of their effectiveness.

(f)   Average the numbers associated responses to the issues you have listed and place this number in the "Actions" side of the fourth circle.

6.   Look at the fifth circle (E). This circle represents your state, region or nation. This will involve people with whom you have no direct relationship, although it may overlap with issues addressed in the earlier parts of this exercise.

(a)   Ask the same questions proposed in 5(a), Substituting local concerns for those confronting your state, region or nation.

(b)   Write "E – State/Region/Nation" at the top of a separate sheet of paper or notebook page. Under this, list the social problems and injustices confronting your state, region or nation. Then, complete the steps outlined in 5(c) through 5(e).

(c)   Average the numbers associated responses to the issues you have listed and place this number in the "Actions" side of the fifth circle.

7.   Look at the outer-most circle (F). This circle represents the world. Again, although it may overlap with issues addressed in the

earlier parts of this exercise, this will involve people with whom you have no direct relationship.

(a) Ask the same questions proposed in 5(a), Substituting local concerns for those confronting the world.

(b) Write "F – World" at the top of a separate sheet of paper or notebook page. Under this, list the social problems and injustices confronting your state, region or nation. Then, complete the steps outlined in 5(c) through 5(e).

(c) Average the numbers associated responses to the issues you have listed and place this number in the "Actions" side of the outer circle.

8. After completing the exercise for the outer-most circle, take time to reflect on the issues listed in each of the circles and the different levels of effectiveness in responding to these concerns. Look for patterns in the diagram as well as in your consideration of the individual issue considered during this exercise. Then, imagine yourself sitting with Jesus and have a conversation with him about these thoughts and any actions they might suggest.

This subsection explores the relationships between three forms a prayer familiar to the ancient Celtic saints: the lament, the litany and the lorica. Each of these types of prayer serves a unique purpose, so take your time exploring them and the ways in which they might help you in your own unique spiritual journey.

The Lament

Part One

The lament is a prayer of loss, sorrow, mourning and even anger. There are many laments found in the Bible, especially among the psalms. Most of these reflect a person's pain or grief (the "individual" psalms of lament) but some also share communal sorrows (the "national" psalms of lament).

These laments, like others found in the Bible (e.g., Ezekiel 33:1-20, Jeremiah 20:7-18, Matthew 3:1-12, etc.) usually follow a similar pattern. They begin by expressing suffering and even a sense of abandonment, often giving a list of events or circumstances causing this pain, before asking for God's help in restoring order. While laments may seem to be complaints, they express the very human struggles of faithful men and women.

Consider, for example, Psalm 12:

> Help, O Lord, for there is no longer anyone who is godly;
>   the faithful have disappeared from humankind.
> They utter lies to each other;
>   with flattering lips and a double heart they speak.
> May the Lord cut off all flattering lips,
>   the tongue that makes great boasts
> those who say, "With our tongues we will prevail;
>   our lips are our own – who is our master?"

"Because the poor are despoiled, because the needy groan,
  I will now rise up," says the Lord;
  "I will place them in the safety for which they long."
The promises of the Lord are promises that are pure,
  silver refined in a furnace on the ground,
  purified seven times.
You, O Lord, will protect us;
  you will guard us from this generation forever.
On every side the wicked prowl,
  as vileness is exalted among humankind.
                                          Psalm 12: 1-8.

After reflecting on this psalm, prayerfully engage it through an imaginative contemplation in which either Ita or Jesus shares the psalm with others. Then, speak with Jesus in your imagination about the meaning of the psalm and how it might connect to your life. Write your observations from this period of prayer in your journal.

Part Two

After finishing your reflections on Psalm 12, on a separate day, look at your diagram from "Circles of Compassion and Action" and find the circle with the lowest number – the issues that were least challenged or resolved. Then, taking as much time (or work sessions) as you need:

1.   Select the largest unaddressed or unresolved issue from the concerns contained in that circle. Then, on separate sheets of paper (or pages in your notebook), write each concern you listed from the topic you have selected. Be as specific as possible, separating each topic into as many distinct and self-contained concerns as possible.

2.   Reflecting on each issue and its related concerns individually, ask… Why was this topic not properly addressed? Was it because of the actions of individual people or groups? Were you part of the reason it was not addressed? What efforts in the past, either by others or by you, sought to solve the problem but proved inadequate? What needs to happen if the problem is to be solved or eliminated?

3.   Again, on separate pages, group your answers from the individual issues into a single list of concerns. This should include the following groupings:

(a)   the reasons why a topic was not properly addressed.

(b)   the actions of people or groups that impeded the resolution of this problem.

(c)   your culpability in Impeding the resolution of this problem.

(d)   the actions by you and others, the sought – but failed – to solve or eliminate the problem.

(e)   future actions needed to solve or eliminate the problem.

4.   In your imagination, prayerfully present these lists to Jesus and discuss them in as much detail as possible. Make certain to note the emotions evoked by each specific issue or response from your lists. When you have finished praying, be certain to include these emotional responses next to each topic for concern.

Part Three

Before writing your lament, take some time to remember:

1.   A lament is a statement of faith in which you expect God to hear you and respond to your needs. You should begin by calling out to God and asking to be heard. Express (or list) the various complaints you have about the failure to resolve the issue at the center of your lament. You should also be able to express your criticism Of God and of those around you in failing to address this issue before.

2.   At the same time, a lament is a statement of pain, suffering, grief and even anger. You are coming before a God who knows every aspect of you, so there is nothing that you are able – or should want – to hide. Present your deepest and truest feelings about this topic as directly and honestly as possible.

3.   Finally, a lament is an affirmation of an existing relationship of love. You have a history of God's loving care and part of the lament should serve as a reminder of the ways in which God has helped you in the past and of your expectation that God will offer loving support for your needs in the present (and the future).

After taking some time reflecting on how these elements of a lament might shape the presentation of the concerns you have, write your prayer. It should include:

1.   a direct appeal to God had its beginning.
2.   a description of the situation, issues or problems which have brought you sorrow or grief.
3.   a specific set of petitions that you are asking God to address.
4.   an affirmation of your trust in God's help (based on your personal or communal history).
5.   a concluding statement of praise.

Note: The form of your lament should be entirely your own. While the psalms and other laments in the Bible are often poems or songs, you should feel free to use whatever style you like. Remember, this is a direct communication between you and a God who knows you better then you know yourself. The words that you share with God should reflect that intimacy.

Part Four

Now, take your lament to prayer. After taking the time you need to focus on the present moment, begin by reading your lament slowly and deliberately. Allow each word and phrase to rest gently in your consciousness and feel the emotions evoked in your reading as you allow yourself to focus entirely on your experiences in the moment. Also, if something does not feel right about your lament (e.g., the wording seems too vague, you find some aspect of a problem out of place, etc.), take the time to rewrite that portion of your prayer.

After prayerfully reading your lament, put all other thoughts out of your consciousness and become as still as possible. Then, return to your lament and read it aloud at the speed that seems most appropriate to the emotions you are trying to convey. Allow yourself to feel the fullness of your grief, sorrow or anger as you speak to God about your needs and desires. When you are finished, imagine Jesus sitting in front of you and speak with him about the specific issues of your lament. As always, make certain to give space for Jesus to respond.

After you have finished these prayers, review your lament and revise any aspects of it that you feel need to be clarified. Then, record your lament and any other significant observations from your prayers in your journal.

The Litany

Part One

Unlike the lament, the litany is a prayer of joyful affirmation. It proclaims the gifts of God's presence in a person's life through a sequence of almost identical statements of faith and gratitude. The repetitive nature of this prayer reaffirms the all-pervasive relationship between God and his creatures by highlighting the various manifestations of God's activity in the life of the person or group praying the litany.

Consider, for example, this litany from the 9th Century *Book of Cerne*:

> Be my helper.
> In the name of the holy Trinity.
> Holy Trinity,
> you are my true God,
> you are my holy Father,
> you are my faithful Lord,
> you are my great King,
> you are my just Judge,
> you are my greatest teacher,
> you are my ready helper,
> you are my powerful physician,
> you are the most excellent of men,
> you are my living bread,
> you are my priest forever,
> you are my leader to the homeland,
> you are my true light,
> you are my sweet holiness,
> you are my perfect patience,
> you are my pure simplicity,
> you are my complete unity,
> you are my peaceful concord,

you are my total care,
you are my safe harbor,
you are my never-ending salvation,
you are my great compassion,
you are my valiant endurance,
you are my spotless offering,
you are my completed redemption,
you are my future hope,
you are my perfect charity,
you are my eternal life, to you I pray,
and ask that I may walk with you
when I rest in you,
and when I rise again before you.
Hear me, O Lord,
who lives and reigns,
now and forever. Amen.

Take a moment to remember Jesus' admonition In Matthew 6:7 that, "When you are praying, do not heap up empty phrases…". Then, reflect on the simplicity of the litany's language and structure. Repetitive spiritual practices may be found in all major religions to achieve various goals, but in the Abrahamic faiths (and certainly among the ancient Celtic saints) the repetitive prayers like the litany must express a person's deepest needs and desires for the prayers to be effective.

With this in mind, after reflecting on this litany, prayerfully engage it in the same manner that you approached your lament – slowly and deliberately at first as you allow each word or phrase to settle into your consciousness and then at the speed that seems most appropriate to the emotions it evokes. Then, add the phrase "to you I pray," to every line that begins "you are my…" and say the litany again at the speed that seems most appropriate to you. Take some time to consider the various emotions and spiritual qualities the litany evokes in you and write your observations in your journal.

Part Two

Again, beginning on a separate day from your reflections on the litany, look at notes you prepared for "Circles of Compassion and Action" and examine the various ways you and other people were able to effectively solve or eliminate the problems you listed. Remember that you achieve them all with God's help, so again taking as much time (or work sessions) as you need:

1.   Group the achievements according to their degree of effectiveness and separate them according to whether they were addressed by individuals or groups. Again, be as specific as possible about the actions that were needed to achieve these results and the people involved in successfully addressing them.

        Note: *You may find it helpful to think about these solutions and achievements in terms of their degree of completion. In this way, there are certain aspects of them for which you can express clear gratitude and others that will be brought to prayer as petitions for the future.*

2.   Reflecting on each issue and its related concerns individually, ask… What aspect of God's activity in the world helped achieve each of these victories? To whom did God offer protection, guidance or initiative in addressing these problems? What more does God need to do who completely solve the problems and concerns found on your lists? What attributes of God will be necessary for these future victories to be achieved?

3.   Then, develop your lists of individual achievements into two lists: one that shows things that have already been achieved and the other activities that need support in the future. Next to each item on each list, write the human quality (e.g., wisdom, courage, patience, etc.) needed for that item either to have been achieved or to be achieved in the future.

4.   In your imagination, prayerfully present these lists and notes to Jesus, discussing them in as much detail as possible. Make certain to note the emotions evoked by each specific issue or response from your lists. When you have finished praying, be certain to include these emotional responses next to each topic for concern.

5.   At the end of your prayer, decide the phrase (or phrases) that you will choose to repeat during your litany. For example, you may decide to use the phrase (e.g., "Lord, source of…", "Grant me…", etc.)

followed by each hopefully qualities you needed to successfully address the problems and issues from "Circles of Compassion and Action".

Part Three

Before writing your litany, take some time to remember:

1.   Like the lament, a litany is a statement of faith in which you expect God to hear you and respond to your needs. You should begin by calling out to God and asking to be heard. Then, recognize that God is the source of all your strengths and capabilities by listing them in a repetitive manner (with or without a responsive phrase). Then, conclude with a simple expression of gratitude or acknowledgement for God's presence in your life.

2.   Also, the litany has tremendous flexibility. For example, you can divide the repetitive strophes into actions or qualities experienced in different times (i.e., past, present and future) with each of these divisions using different invocational phrases. You also have the freedom to include or exclude responses to your invocational phrases (see the final paragraph of Part One of this consideration of the litany).

3.   Finally, as with all prayer, a litany affirms an existing relationship of love. You have a history of God's loving care and part of the lament should serve as a reminder of the ways in which God has helped you in the past and of your expectation that God will offer loving support for your needs in the present (and the future).

After taking some time reflecting on how these elements of a litany might shape the presentation of the concerns you have, write your prayer. It should include:
1.   a direct appeal to God had its beginning.
2.   the invocational phrase (or phrases) that you will choose to repeat during your litany. For example, you may decide to use the phrase (e.g., "Lord, source of...", "Grant me...", etc.) followed by each hopefully qualities you needed to successfully address the problems and issues from "Circles of Compassion and Action".
3.   responsive phrase(s) to your invocations, if you choose to include any. These could be a single repeated phrase (e.g., "Grant us

your grace", Help us", etc.) or phrases that respond specifically to the attribute mentioned in the invocation. (e.g., "courage… Grant us bravery", wisdom… Grant us insight", etc.)

4.   a concluding statement of praise.

Part Four

Now, take your litany to prayer. After taking the time you need to focus on the present moment, begin by reading your litany slowly and deliberately. Allow each word and phrase to rest gently in your consciousness and feel the emotions evoked in your reading as you allow yourself to focus entirely on your experiences in the moment. Also, if something does not feel right about your litany (e.g., the wording seems too vague, you find some aspect of a problem out of place, etc.), take the time to rewrite that portion of your prayer.

After prayerfully reading your litany, put all other thoughts out of your consciousness and become as still as possible. Then, return to your lament and read it aloud at the speed that seems most appropriate to the emotions you are trying to convey. Allow yourself to feel the fullness of your joy as you invoke God's presence by speaking of how the various divine attribute have fulfilled (and will fulfill) your various needs and desires.

After you have finished these prayers, review your litany and revise any aspects of it that you feel need to be clarified. Then, record your lament and any other significant observations from your prayers in your journal.

The Lorica

Part One

Often referred to in the Celtic tradition as a breastplate, the lorica is a prayer of protection. It very directly and deliberately asks for gods care and shielding in a world which can be hostile both to God's desires and to those who seek to serve God in the world. It is a highly personal prayer, so it can take depending upon the person invoking it.

72

Consider, for example, this anonymous lorica found on a 10th Century manuscript:

> May our Lord Jesus Christ
> be near you to defend you,
> within you to refresh you,
> around you to preserve you,
> before you to guide you,
> behind you to justify you,
> above you to bless you;
> who lives and reigns
> with the Father and the Holy Spirit,
> one God, now and forever.

This lorica is a caim, also called an "encircling prayer". In this case, the prayer is being said as a blessing upon another person as it asks God to protectively surround that person in a dangerous world. However, the caim also may be used to invoke God's protection for the person saying the prayer or for significant objects or events.

Now, consider the 7th Century Lorica of St. Fursa (Fursey):

> May the guiding hands of God be on my shoulders,
> may the presence of the Holy Spirit be on my head,
> may the sign of Christ be on my forehead,
> may the voice of the Holy Spirit be in my ears,
> may the smell of the Holy Spirit be in my nose,
> may the sight of the company of heaven be in my eyes,
> may the speech of the company of heaven be in my mouth,
> may the work of the church of God be in my hands,
> may the serving of God and my neighbor be in my feet,
> may God make my heart his home,
> and may I belong to God, my Father, completely.

In this case, the lorica (which you may recognize since it was used incorporated into the morning and evening prayers of the second section) blesses the person with God's protection using language that mirrors the anointing an individual would receive when going out into the world on mission. So, it is not surprising this particular lorica amplifies this liturgical imagery by using a repetitive pattern very much like the litany.

> *Note: You also may find it useful to consider the most famous Celtic lorica: Saint Patrick's Breastplate, also known as "The Deer's Cry". Much longer than the examples presented above, it incorporates many different types of Celtic prayer in a single statement of faith as it invokes God's protection at the beginning of the day. Many translations (including a particularly eloquent one by Kuno Meyer) are available online.*

After considering these prayers, take time to prayerfully engage each of them in turn on separate days. On each day, begin by saying the lorica slowly and deliberately, allowing each word and phrase to settle to settle into your consciousness. Then, reread the prayer again at the speed that seems most appropriate to you. Afterward, take time to reflect on the dynamics of this prayer in relation to your own spiritual needs and prayer style. Finally, share your reflections in an imaginary conversation with Jesus and write your observations in your journal.

Part Two

After these considerations, prepare a lorica of your own by considering the challenges that you are confronting that require God's protection and the style a prayer that best suits your temperament. You may find it helpful to review your notes from "Circles of Compassion and Action" to answer the first concern and the notes you have written in your journal concerning the lament, the litany and the lorica.

Begin by considering your personal or social situation. Ask… What are the various ways that you need God's protection, both in your daily life and in moments of particular stress? Do you feel especially threatened by any particular circumstances in your life? Are there specific men or women That you feel are trying to harm you? If so, what are they doing and how can God protect you from these actions? How might you be harming yourself and how might God protect you from these actions?

Then, decide on the style of your lorica. Take a moment to consider how you experience God's presence in your life and think of the prayer style that comes closest to mirroring your encounters with God. If you feel God embracing you in moments of crisis, you might want to prepare a caim. On the other hand, if you experience God as a pervasive presence that takes particular form according to the specific needs of the moment, then you might consider a litany. Finally, if you feel particularly threatened, you might consider modeling your lorica on a lament, perhaps mirroring Psalms 3 or 5.

Finally, write your lorica. Decide if any of the various examples of prayer described in this subsection inspire you, even going online to research them in more detail if necessary. Also, think about any personally significant biblical verses that you might be able to adapt into a lorica. Allow your mind to freely play with the styles of prayer as they interact with the needs you have for God's protection. Then, finally, write the lorica that seems best suited to you, your personal needs and your temperament. Whether it is long or short, it should be something that you want to pray on a daily basis – at least until your circumstances change.

Part Three

Now, take your lorica to prayer. After taking the time you need to focus on the present moment, begin by reading your lorica slowly and deliberately. Allow each word and phrase to rest gently in your consciousness and feel the emotions evoked in your reading as you allow yourself to focus entirely on your experiences in the moment. Also, if something does not feel right about your prayer (e.g., the wording seems too vague, you find some aspect of a problem out of place, etc.), take the time to rewrite that portion.

After prayerfully reading your lorica, put all other thoughts out of your consciousness and become as still as possible. Then, return to your prayer and read it aloud at the speed that seems most appropriate to the emotions you are trying to convey. Allow yourself to feel the fullness of your joy as you invoke God's presence and protection.

After you have finished these prayers, review your lorica and revise any aspects of it that you feel need to be clarified. Then, record your lament and any other significant observations from your prayers in your journal.

The exercises of this section expand on your retreat experiences during "(IX) The Promised Land of the Saints & The Return Home" in A Pilgrimage to the Land of the Saints. *Before proceeding to the following reflections and prayers, it might be helpful to review "Treasuring the Gifts of Pilgrimage" following "(IX) The Promised Land of the Saints & The Return Home" in the first section of* A Journey to the Land of the Saints.

Living as a child of God transforms both you and the world around you, bringing gifts of joy and companionship you are meant to share with others. Whether through your actions or your words, you are called to invite others to enter your world so they may experience the same blessings as you. This act of hospitality makes God's divine love tangible through human actions and behaviors.

So, take a moment to consider Chester Kallman's translation of "St. Ita's Vision":

> "I will take nothing from my Lord," said she,
> "unless He gives me His Son from Heaven
> In the form of a Baby that I may nurse Him".
> So that Christ came down to her
> in the form of a Baby and then she said:
> "Infant Jesus, at my breast,
> Nothing in this world is true
> Save, O tiny nursling, You.
> Infant Jesus at my breast,
> By my heart every night,
> You I nurse are not a churl
> But were begot on Mary the Jewess
> By Heaven's light.
> Infant Jesus at my breast,
> What King is there but You who could
> Give everlasting good?
> Wherefore I give my food.

Sing to Him, maidens, sing your best!
There is none that has such right
To your song as Heaven's King
Who every night
Is Infant Jesus at my breast."

Note: Chester Kallman's translation of "St. Ita's Vision" was used in Samuel Barber's *Hermit Songs*, a collection of ancient Celtic poems set to music. While Samuel Barber's music is not Celtic in style, his interpretation of "St. Ita's Vision" (especially the version sung by Leontyne Price) highlights its seminal aspects.

While these verses may be St. Ita's own composition, they usually are attributed to an anonymous Irish monk who lived between the 8th and 13th Centuries. Regardless of the true author, this song reveals aspects of Ita's personality and vocation that deserve deeper reflection.

While Barber prepared these poems as modern

Begin by using one session reflecting on the following points:

1.   While Ita was called the "foster-mother of saints" she was never a actual mother. The young children she nurtured were not infants when they arrived at her community. Yet, in every other sense of the word she became their mother as she guided them and nurtured their faith so that they would be prepared to enter other communities in the service of God.

2.   Ita may have prayed (or been depicted by a future monk as praying) with the most intimate image of motherhood available to reinforce the deep love between Ita and the children in her care (as well with God, her sustainer). It also is an aspect of motherhood Ita never experienced and may have desired.

3.   Nursing is a mutual exchange between mother and child. While the mother provides nourishment, the act of nursing reinforces the bond between mother and child as well as provides comfort to both.

Note: Many great saints and mystics have used the experiences of others, including those which were beyond their own human capabilities, to express their incompleteness and neediness before God. The 16th Century John of the Cross, for example, once depicted his soul as a bride seeking her lost bridegroom.

4.   Intimacy is essential to effective Christian witness. Although it is important to use discretion by balancing openness against prudent caution, the act of giving witness involves a form of spiritual hospitality in which men and women invite others into their world of faith so they may express the deepest aspects of their spiritual experiences.

With this in mind, consider the following questions:

1.   What is your personal reaction to "St. Ita's Vision"? Do you find yourself drawn to its imagery?... Or disturbed by it?... Or distanced from it? Be as specific as possible in pointing to particular lines or moments in the poem that attract or bother you.

2.   Has "St. Ita's Vision" become dated or does it retain its vitality centuries after it was written? If it is dated, how might it be revised to address a modern audience? If it retains its vitality, what do you think are the elements of the poem that seem most important to contemporary readers or listeners?

3.   How does "St. Ita's Vision" communicate the inner journey of the Celtic monk or nun? How does this compare to the story of Brendan's epic pilgrimage? How do these very different images relate to one another? How do each help you understand the spiritual lives of the ancient Celtic saints?

4.   Does the use of the imagination by the ancient Celtic saints inspire you share your own faith or spiritual experiences to some form of creative expression? If so, what form might that take?

Again, linger on any questions that seem especially significant and bring these concerns to your subsequent prayer.

Articulate witness, sharing of your faith with others, serves to strengthen the faith of those who already believe and open nonbelievers to God's love. Aided by the Holy Spirit, effective witness flows through the confluence of personal passions – emerging from your most powerful experiences of God's love and grace – and a careful consideration of the creative tools available to express those passions.

Note: Articulate witness is not about apologetics or the defense of doctrinal issues. It involves the creation of clear and cogent demonstrations of faith capable of capturing the imagination of others, whether fellow believers or strangers to faith. Sometimes, it also may offer intelligent and empathetic conversations about religious faith and doubt in the damaged world in which we live.

With this in mind, take some time to complete the following exercises exploring personal passion, style and voice.

Part One:

The beginning of Christian witness begins with the exploration of your deepest passions and most intimate spiritual experiences. By knowing what you care about, as well as by learning your inhibitions in sharing these feelings and events with others, you will become a better witness to God's love to the world around you. The idea of giving witness to your faith in a public manner may disturb or even frighten you, so it is important that you take time to understand your own reluctance before recognizing that God will never ask you to do something without first giving you the gifts needed to achieve success.

So, with this in mind, use one session to…

1.   Begin by considering one of your most intimate and pleasant experiences. In your imagination, allow the physical sensations and memories of this completely private and joyful moment to ebb and flow in your consciousness.

2.   Then, imagine yourself in an open public space. See a stranger approach you and here that person asking you to tell them about the moment you just experienced. See your reaction and hear your

response to that stranger. Afterward, allow these images to fade away before reflecting on the emotions you have just experienced.

3.   Next, imagine yourself speaking with a close friend or family member in a quiet and private place. As the conversation turns to special moments in both of your lives, hear your friend or family member ask about your most intimate experience. Again, see your reaction and hear your response to your friend or family member. Afterward, allow these images to fade away before reflecting on the emotions you have just experienced.

4.   Finally, imagine yourself speaking with Jesus in the same space you just shared with your close friend or family member. Here Jesus ask you about your most important an intimate experience of God's love. Again, see your reaction and hear your response to Jesus' question. See and hear Jesus' reply, asking you to share your most important experience of God's love with others.

5.   While still in conversation with Jesus, explain your willingness and your reluctance to share such an intimate moment of God's love with others. See and hear Jesus respond to each issue in turn, expressing his understanding and support. As Jesus fades from your consciousness, hear yourself agree with his request. Take a moment to reflect on the emotions you experienced during your conversations with Jesus.

6.   Next, imagine yourself speaking with a close friend or family member in the quiet and private place from earlier. Tell that close friend or family member about your most intimate and pleasurable experience of God's love. See his or her reaction and hear his or her response to your words. Afterward, allow these images to fade away before reflecting on the emotions you have just experienced.

7.   Then, imagine yourself in the public space from before and see the stranger talking with you. As the conversation turns to issues of God and sin, tell the stranger about your most intimate experience of God's love. See the stranger's reaction and hear the stranger's response to your words. Afterward, allow these images to fade away before reflecting on the emotions you have just experienced.

8.   Conclude this session by allowing the physical sensations and memories of this exercise to ebb and flow in your consciousness. As these feelings and images fade, reflect on any guidance you have received through your conversations with the stranger, your close friend or family member, and Jesus. Afterward, record your thoughts in your journal

Part Two:

You have many ways to express yourself, your passions and your spiritual experiences to others, and your choice of one form of expression over another is a matter of style – something which makes you distinctive but not necessarily unique. Your expressive style usually emerges from the recognition that it allows you to better articulate your thoughts and feelings to others – or that it best fits your personality. Still, while you may already have a preference for one type of expression, it would be useful for you to consider different ways to express yourself since you might discover aspects of yourself which you have hitherto not known.

With this in mind, complete the following exercise taking as much time as you need.

1.   Review the stories of Ita in "Nurturing the Courage of Pilgrims" and the story of Canair in "Sacred Citizenship and the Challenge of Hope". Then, using your journal notes surrounding the stories, select the one you find most interesting or spiritually rewarding to read.

2.   Rewrite the story you selected, transposing it into the modern world. Do not be afraid to change details from the original story as you make it relevant to a modern reader. Instead, focus on its essential message concerning Ita or Canair and their relationship with God. Reflect on the pleasures and challenges of writing the story after you are finished, recording these thoughts in your journal.

3.   Rework the story as a poem. Do not worry about rhyme or structure unless this is important to you. If so, review the structural requirements of the type of poem you want to write. Again, record the pleasures and challenges of this experience in your Journal when you have finished.

Note: If you have musical skills, transform your poem into a song or develop a way to present your poem in a musical context.

4.   Reconceive the story without words:

      (a)   Use a visual or performing art. This might be a wordless cartoon sequence, a photo essay (using either your own images or some found on the internet), a drawing or painting, a sculpture in clay or a dance. Unless you have already developed skills in one of these areas, do not worry about the quality of the work. Instead, focus on expressing yourself through these tools. When you have finished, record your thoughts on this experience in your journal.

      (b)   Use a craft. This might be a collage, a quilt or some type of embroidery. Again, unless you have a special skill in one of these areas, you should focus on expressing yourself through whichever craft you choose. Again, record your thoughts in your journal when you are finished.

5.   Review your journal notes after completing these various projects in a single prayer session. Reflectively look at your work and compare your experiences with each. Bring these thoughts to Jesus in prayer through an imagined conversation about each item you created. Remember to say a short prayer of gratitude at the end of this prayer session.

6.   Finally, decide if there are any of these creations that you would like to share with others. If so, develop a plan for their presentation – through a reading or performance, through a gallery exhibition or through social media.

Part Three:

Voice is not about the way you express yourself. Instead, it is about how you become part of the expression. Even if you have a similar style to others, and use the same tools as they do, you will not use them in the same manner nor will the message you convey be the same as any other person. Once you achieve this sense of uniqueness, you will be able to give witness to your faith in a manner that becomes entirely your own and you will be able to welcome others Into a unique experience of God's love that serves and assists the unfolding plan of redemption.

With this in mind, after retelling a story of Ita or Canair, tell a story of yourself by completing the following exercise, again taking as much time as you need.

1.   Reflect on one of your most powerful experiences of God's love. Consider how it changed your life, strengthening your faith and gave your confidence to approach God in prayer. Then, bring these thoughts to Jesus in prayer through an imagined conversation about this experience and its significance in your life. Remember to say a short prayer of gratitude at the end of this prayer session.

2.   Write a short statement about your experience explaining its important to your spiritual life and faith. Prepare this for a receptive audience, one you know will affirm and support you as you share this very important moment in your life with them. As you write, take note of your joys and worries you feel at the prospect of revealing this private moment with others. When you are finished, record the pleasures and challenges of preparing this statement in your journal.

3.   Rework the statement you prepared as a story or poem, either from your own perspective or someone else. Choose the audience for this story or poem, deciding which genre of writing best meets the needs of these readers. Then, focus on the essential aspects of your experience these readers need to understand as you write your story or poem. Again, record the pleasures and challenges of this experience in your Journal when you have finished.

    Note: *Again, if you have musical skills, you might decide to transform your poem into a song or develop a way to present your poem in a musical context.*

4.   Reconceive your story or poem without words using a visual art, a performing art for a craft. When choosing which of these tools to use, review your notes from the last exercise and select the art or craft which gave you the deepest feelings of personal happiness and accomplishment. Again, focus on expressing yourself through

whichever tool you choose. Again, when you have finished, record your thoughts on this experience in your journal.

5.　　　Review your journal notes after completing these various projects in a single prayer session. Reflectively look at your work and compare your experiences with each. Bring these thoughts to Jesus in prayer through an imagined conversation about item you have created. Remember to say a short prayer of gratitude at the end of this prayer session.

6.　　　Finally, decide if there are any of these creations that you would like to share with others. If so, develop a plan for their presentation – through a reading or performance, through a gallery exhibition or through social media.

As you go out into the world as witnesses to God's love, may you always remember this adaptation of an ancient Celtic prayer:

> My speech and my action – may it praise you without
> flaw: May my heart love you, King of heaven
> and earth.
> My speech and my action – may it praise you without
> flaw: Make it easy for me, pure Lord, to do you
> all service and to adore you.
> My speech and my action – may it praise you without
> flaw: Father of all affection, hear my poems
> and my speech.

Preparing a Personal Penitential

The exercises of this section expand on your retreat experiences during "(IV) The Paradise of Birds" in A Pilgrimage to the Land of the Saints. *Before proceeding to the following reflections and prayers, it might be helpful to review "Accepting Forgiveness as a Loved Sinner" following "(IV) The Paradise of Birds" in the first section of* A Journey to the Land of the Saints.

Living as "colonies of heaven", the ancient Celtic saints were especially concerned with the effects of sin on the life of faith. Repentance and penance were central to their spiritual practices since any form of sinful behavior was seen as an impediment to living as "citizens of heaven". However, they also understood that forgiveness is an essential aspect of Christ's ongoing mission of redemption. As such, they embraced both the sorrow begotten of our sin and the joy received through God's redemptive love.

This duality is expressed most clearly in the manuals used by the ancient Celtic saints to govern their practices of confessing sins and imposing penances for the forgiveness of these sins. Called penitentials, these books often prescribed specific – and sometimes quite harsh – penalties for various types of sinful behavior. Yet, the goal of these penances was not merely punishment. For the Celtic saints, the purpose of these penitential penalties was to help the repentant sinner develop habits of behavior that avoided future sinful actions.

With these thoughts in mind, it might be helpful for you to develop your own personal penitential manual.

Note: You may want to include this penitential in your retreat journal. However, since it is meant to provide you with ongoing guidance, you might find it more helpful to use another notebook for it. In this way, you will be able to access it easily and carry it with you when you travel.

Part One

Before preparing your penitential, it is important for you to come to an appreciation of the emotional dynamics of sin and forgiveness, an intermingling of sorrow and joy. This experience is perhaps demonstrated most clearly in what is known as the "gift of tears". The tears of repentant sinners express the sorrow men and women feel after alienating themselves from God – and from their true nature as children of God – but these tears also become a reminder the salvific water a baptism that washed away sin.

Now, in a single session, bring these thoughts to prayer.

1.   After taking the time you need to focus on the present moment, begin by reading the following anonymous poem slowly and deliberately. Allow each word and phrase to rest gently in your consciousness and feel the emotions evoked in your reading as you allow yourself to focus entirely on your experiences in the moment. Allow yourself to pause between words and phrases to express your own prayers to God.

> Grant me tears, O Lord, to blot out my sins; may I not cease from them, O God, until I have been purified.
> May my heart be burned by the fire of redemption; grant me pure tears for Mary and Ita.
> When I contemplate my sins, grant me tears always, for great are the claims of tears on cheeks.
> Grant me tears when rising, grant me tears when resting, beyond your every gift all together for love with you, Mary's son.
> Grant me tears in bed to moisten my pillow, so that his dear ones may help to cure the soul.
> Grant me contrition of hard so that I may not be in disgrace; O Lord, protect me and grant me tears.
> For the dalliance I had with (wo)men, who did not reject me, grant me tears, O Creator, flowing in streams from my eyes.

For my anger, my jealousy, and my pride, a foolish
 deed, in pools from my inmost parts bring
 forth tears.
My falsehoods, my lying, and my greed, grievous the
 three, to banish them all from me, O Mary,
 grant me tears.

2.   Remaining prayerful, read the following selection from *The
Spiritual Exercises of Saint Ignatius of Loyola*:

> True spiritual consolation may be known by the
> following signs. A certain interior impulse raises the
> soul towards the Creator, makes it love Him with an
> ardent love and no longer permits it to love any other
> creature but for Him; sometimes gentle tears cause
> this love, tears that flow from repentance of past faults
> or the sight of the sorrows of Jesus Christ or any other
> motive that enlightened religion inspires; finally, all
> that increases faith, hope, charity; all that fills the soul
> with holy joy, makes it more attached to meditation
> on heavenly things and more careful of salvation; all
> that leads it to find repose and peace in the Lord – all
> this is true and spiritual consolation.
>
> Spiritual Exercises, #316

3.   Now, imagine Jesus standing or sitting in front of you. Read the
previous passage concerning tears together and speak to one another
about the meaning of the various words and phrases of the passage.
Ask Jesus to help you better understand the consoling nature of tears.
As always, allow Jesus to guide the conversation. At the end of your
conversation, ask that you may receive tears – with both joy and sorrow
– as you repent your sins.

4.   Record any significant thoughts or observations from your prayers
in your journal.

On a separate day, approach Luke 7:36-50 as an imaginative contemplation.

1.   Either from the woman's perspective or paying specific attention to the woman of this story, see Simon the Pharisee's house and the people in it (i.e., Jesus, Simon and the other guests). Observe the reactions of everyone, including Jesus, as she enters and begins to wash Jesus' feet. Hear Jesus tell the parable of the debtors and his explanation of the story to Simon. Watch as Jesus forgives the woman, noting her response and the reaction of the other people in the house.

2.   Allow this scene to fade from your consciousness, holding onto the emotions you experienced during your contemplation of Jesus at Simon the Pharisee's house. In your imagination, see Jesus sitting or standing in front of you and bring your thoughts to him in conversation. Again, allow Jesus to guide the conversation.

3.   When you are finished, record any significant thoughts or observations from your prayers in your journal.

Part Two

The path to redemptive forgiveness begins with humility and sorrow. These feelings are graces given by God that open us to accept the pain through our separation from God and the humble acceptance that this loss results from our own misguided choices. So, as you begin to prepare your personal penitential, you should begin by considering prayers of contrition that allow you to express the sorrow you experience from your sins and the humility with which you are now approaching God in the hope of forgiveness.

With this in mind, in a single prayer session, bring this traditional Celtic act of contrition ro prayer.

1.   After taking the time you need to focus on the present moment, begin by reading the following prayer from the *Carmina Gadelica* slowly and deliberately. Allow each word and phrase to rest gently in your consciousness and feel the emotions evoked in your reading as you allow yourself to focus entirely on your experiences in the moment.

Allow yourself to pause between words and phrases to express your own prayers to God.

> Jesu, give me forgiveness of sins,
> Jesu, keep my guilt in my memory,
> Jesu, give me the grace of repentance,
> Jesu, give me the grace of forgiveness,
> Jesu, give me the grace of submission,
> Jesu, give me the grace of earnestness,
> Jesu, give me the grace of lowliness,
> To make a free confession at this time,
> To condemn myself at the chair of confession
> Lest I be condemned at the chair of judgment;
> Jesu, give me strength and courage
> To condemn myself at the chair of confession
> Lest I be condemned at the chair of judgment.
> It is easier for me to go under subjection for a brief while
> Than to go to death during eternity.
> Jesu, give me to confess my guilt
> As earnestly as were this the moment of my death.

> Jesu, take pity upon me,
> Jesu, have mercy upon me,
> Jesu, take me to Thee,
> Jesu, aid my soul.

Carmina Gadelica, #296.

2.   Now, imagine Jesus standing or sitting in front of you. Say the prayer to him and ask about the meaning of the various words and phrases of the in the prayer. When you are finished, speak with Jesus about the specific issues of repentance and contrition. Again, allow Jesus to guide the conversation.

3.   After your prayer, record any significant thoughts or observations from your prayers in your journal.

On another day, in a single session, bring these thoughts Psalm 51:1-12 to prayer.

1. After taking the time you need to focus on the present moment, begin by reading Psalm 51:1-12 slowly and deliberately. Allow each word and phrase to rest gently in your consciousness and feel the emotions evoked in your reading as you allow yourself to focus entirely on your experiences in the moment. Allow yourself to pause between words and phrases to express your own prayers to God.

> Have mercy on me, O God,
>   according to your steadfast love;
> according to your abundant mercy
>   blot out my transgressions.
> Wash me thoroughly from my iniquity,
>   and cleanse me from my sin.
> For I know my transgressions,
>   and my sin is ever before me.
> Against you, you alone, have I sinned,
>   and done what is evil in your sight,
> so that you are justified in your sentence
>   and blameless when you pass judgment.
> Indeed, I was born guilty,
>   a sinner when my mother conceived me.
> You desire truth in the inward being;
>   therefore teach me wisdom in my secret heart.
> Purge me with hyssop, and I shall be clean;
>   wash me, and I shall be whiter than snow.
> Let me hear joy and gladness;
>   let the bones that you have crushed rejoice.
> Hide your face from my sins,
>   and blot out all my iniquities.
> Create in me a clean heart, O God,
>   and put a new and right spirit within me.
> Do not cast me away from your presence,
>   and do not take your holy spirit from me.
> Restore to me the joy of your salvation,
>   and sustain in me a willing spirit.
>
>   Psalm 51: 1-12

2. Now, imagine Jesus standing or sitting in front of you. Read the psalm together and speak about the meaning of the various words and

phrases of the in it. Again, speak with Jesus about the specific issues of repentance and contrition, allowing Jesus to guide the conversation.

3.   After your prayer, record any significant thoughts or observations from your prayers in your journal.

On a separate day, look at your notebook for this penitential and divide it into nine equal sections. Label the beginning of the first section "Contrition" and write the prayer from the *Carmina Gadelica* and the selection from Psalm 51 under that heading. If you know any other prayers of contrition – either from your own denomination or from other sources – write them in this section as well.

In the future, add different prayers of contrition to this section of your penitential as you encounter them. You may find it helpful to use different prayers at different times, both to avoid allowing your prayer to become routine and to express differently your sense of sorrow when confessing specific sins.

Part Three

Embracing the grace of contrition gives you the courage to approach God as you confess your sins. It is important to remember God loves you and wants to forgive you, so it is also important that you be as humble and open as possible when confessing your sinful actions. God already knows all of your transgressions and is waiting for you to acknowledge them before asking for forgiveness.

To better understand this, approach Luke 18:9-14 as an imaginative contemplation.

1.   Listen to Jesus as he tells the parable of the pharisee and the tax collector. See Jesus with a group of people, either from a distance or close to Jesus. Note whether the group is large or small as well as if the group is inside or outside. Observe whether Jesus is speaking to his disciples or to strangers. Hear Jesus tell the parable and allow the story

to unfold in your mind before watching the reaction of the group to parable.

2.   Allow this scene to fade from your consciousness, holding onto the emotions you experienced during your contemplation of the parable of the pharisee and the tax collector. In your imagination, see Jesus sitting or standing in front of you and bring your thoughts to him in conversation. Again, allow Jesus to guide the conversation into the issues of sorrow, humility and contrition.

3.   When you are finished, record any significant thoughts or observations from your prayers in your journal.

On a separate day, in a single session, reflect on the following concerns as you continue to prepare your personal penitential.

1.   Consider the following excerpts from the Penitential of Cummean, (who, like Brendan, was a foster-child of Ita):

(a)   "He who steals someone else's property by any means shall restore four times as much to him who he has injured."

(b)   "He who incapacitates or maims a man with a blow in a quarrel shall meet his medical expenses and shall make good damages for the injury and shall do his work until he has recovered and shall do penance for half a year. If he does not have the resources to make restitution for these things, he shall do penance for one year."

(c)   "A priest or Deacon who commits natural fornication... shall do penance for seven years. He shall ask pardon every hour and shall perform a special fast every week."

Note: *Notice that Cummean's penitential emphasizes both the repair of the human problems – sometimes in a manner going beyond proportional justice, such as in the case of stealing -- caused by sin as well as specific actions designed to remind the person of the sin he or she committed and to foster better spiritual habits. These are essential aspects of Celtic spirituality that need to be incorporated into your own personal penitential.*

2.   Reflect on the Seven Deadly Sins as they relate to your own life experience: pride, greed, envy, wrath, lust, gluttony and sloth.

(a)   Consider the general effects of each type of sin. Consider...

(i)   **Pride**, usually regarded as the most serious of the Seven Deadly Sins, places an individual at the center of the universe. It denies the importance of all others, including God and our fellow creatures. By subverting humility and modesty, it diminishes our capacities for reverence and respectful behavior.

(II)   **Greed** emerges from a desire to possess more than we need. It makes the acquisition of material goods more important than our relationships with others, including God. It undermines our capacities for benevolence, generosity and sacrifice.

(iii)   **Envy** begets a resentful covetousness toward the gifts of others (such as personality traits or possessions) and undermines a person's awareness of their own giftedness. This simmering dissatisfaction severs human relationships and diminishes the capacity for kindness, compassion and joy.

(iv)   **Wrath** evokes uncontrolled feelings of anger and even hatred toward others. It seeks vengeance at the expense of justice while also undermining the human capacities for forgiveness and mercy.

(v)   **Lust** leads to the disordered love of individuals. It diminishes our capacity to recognize and love others as we objectify them. Generally regarded as the least offensive of the Seven Deadly Sins, lust diminishes our capacity for to act towards others with the purity of intention required of children of God.

(vi)   **Gluttony** involves overindulgence and waste, usually focused on food. However, it also involves any excessive desire that deprives others of their needs. As such, gluttony is an act of selfishness that places a person's concerns, impulses or interests above the well-being of others.

(vii)   **Sloth** goes beyond laziness, leading a person to become indifferent towards his or her own life as well as those of others. Its indolence leads to passivity, apathy and rancor. It subverts the diligence and persistence necessary to live a good life in harmony with God's desires.

(b)   Consider the effects of each type of sin on you, deciding which sins tempt you the most and which tempt you the least. Remember that sinful behavior changes. You may have overcome certain temptations, only to find that other sins become more attractive.

So, be attentive to your entire personal history and all the sins you have committed throughout your life (or at least as many as possible)..

(c) Consider specific sinful actions that emerge from these sins and how they affect you, the people you know and the people you do not know.

(d) Consider the specific sinful actions that emerge from these sins that affect the non-human parts of creation.

Note: *Take as much time as you need for this consideration of the* Seven Deadly Sins. *You may also find it useful to return to this set of reflections in the future as you expand you're penitential.*

3. In your penitential notebook, label the second through eighth sections for the Seven Deadly Sins. Either use the order I provided above or list them according to the degree of influence each sin has on you, beginning with the one that tempts you the most and ending with the least tempting. Then, divide the sections for each sin into four equal subsections and label them "Self", "Family and Friends", "Strangers" and "Creation".

4. List specific sinful actions or transgressions in your penitential, grouping them according to the specific deadly sin involved and the person or thing hurt by that sin (i.e. you, your family or friends, strangers, creation). Make the description of each sin as succinct and specific as possible (e.g., lying to a friend, envying a coworker, etc.) and attach a corresponding penance that includes:

(a) a human action intended to repair the effects of the sin (e.g., apologizing, paying for any damage, etc.).

(b) the number of times a penitential action should be repeated (e.g., each day for a week, every morning for a month, etc.).

(c) additional penances (e.g., fasting, saying special prayers, etc.) you feel will help you remember the pain of the sin.

Note: *The entry for each sin might be something like, "For hurtfully mocking a friend, apologize. Then, repent each day for the following month. Say a prayer of contrition at the beginning of each week of that month."*

5. Develop a short formula of repentance (e.g., "For the sin of [state sin], forgive this sinner.") to be used during your confession and as part

of your penance afterward. Both when confessing and repenting again later as a penance, bring your sin into your consciousness by breathing in deeply. Then, release your breath slowly and say the formula with a heart-felt awareness of the sin you committed.

When using this penitential during confession, begin by allowing all other thoughts and concerns to fall away and focus on the consideration of your sins. Then, begin with an examination of consciousness as you reflect on the period since your last confession. Bring each sinful action into focus and find the corresponding send in your penitential before confessing your sin using the formula of repentance. Afterward, give yourself time to accept the forgiveness of God as your sin Is absolved.

Note: It is important to remember that while your sin has been forgiven in the moment of your confession, the penance you enact afterward is intended to remind you of your past behavior and help you to avoid sinful actions in the future.

Part Four

With your sins now forgiven, you return to your daily life with joy. Restored to your rightful place as a child of God, you again experience the fullness of God's love. You feel the protection and guidance that your relationship with God offers, and you should express that sense of joyful trust in prayers of gratitude and assurance.

With this in mind, in A single session, ring Psalm 23:1-6 to prayer.

1.   After taking the time you need to focus on the present moment, begin by reading Psalm 23:1-6 slowly and deliberately. Allow each word and phrase to rest gently in your consciousness and feel the emotions evoked in your reading as you allow yourself to focus entirely on your experiences in the moment. Allow yourself to pause between words and phrases to express your own prayers to God.

The Lord is my shepherd, I shall not want.

He makes me lie down in green pastures;
he leads me beside still waters;
    he restores my soul.
He leads me in right paths
    for his name's sake.

Even though I walk through the darkest valley,
    I fear no evil;
for you are with me;
    your rod and your staff –
    they comfort me.
You prepare a table before me
    in the presence of my enemies;
you anoint my head with oil;
    my cup overflows.
Surely goodness and mercy shall follow me
    all the days of my life,
and I shall dwell in the house of the Lord
    my whole life long.

                Psalm 23: 1-6

2.   Now, imagine Jesus standing or sitting in front of you. Read the psalm together and speak about the meaning of the various words and phrases of the in it. Again, speak with Jesus about your trust in God's guidance and protection, allowing Jesus to guide the conversation.

3.   After your prayer, record any significant thoughts or observations from your prayers in your journal.

On another day, in a single session, bring these this prayer from the *Carmina Gadelica* to prayer.

1.   After taking the time you need to focus on the present moment, begin by reading the following prayer from the *Carmina Gadelica* slowly and deliberately. Allow each word and phrase to rest gently in your consciousness and feel the emotions evoked in your reading as you allow yourself to focus entirely on your experiences in the moment. Allow yourself to pause between words and phrases to express your own prayers to God.

God to enfold me,
God to surround me,
God in my speaking,
God in my thinking.

God in my sleeping,
God in my waking,
God in my watching,
God in my hoping.

God in my life,
God in my lips,
God in my hands,
God in my heart.

God in my sufficing,
God in my slumber,
God in mine ever-living soul,
God in mine eternity.

Carmina Gadelica, #231

2.   Now, imagine Jesus standing or sitting in front of you. Say the prayer together. When you are finished, speak with Jesus about your trust in God's guidance and protection, allowing Jesus to guide the conversation.

3.   After your prayer, record any significant thoughts or observations from your prayers in your journal.

On a separate day, look at your notebook for this penitential and divide it into nine equal sections. Label the beginning of the final section "Joyful Trust" and write the prayer from the *Carmina Gadelica* and Psalm 23 under that heading. If you know any other prayers of joyful trust, write them in this section as well.

In the future, add different prayers of joyful trust to this section of your penitential as you encounter them. Like the prayers of contrition, you may find it helpful to use different prayers at different times, both to avoid allowing your prayer to become routine and to express differently your joy at being forgiven and your trust in God's future guidance.

Part Five

Having prepared your personal penitential, it is time for you to confess your sins using it. Begin by allowing all of your daily concerns to fall away so that you may be completely alone with God. Then...

1.   In a slow and deliberate manner, say your prayer of contrition. Allow each word and phrase to linger in your consciousness and evoke the sorrow and humility needed to approach God.

2.   Take time to carefully consider your various sins and the effect they have had on Your life and your relationship with God. Allow your sorrow to enter your consciousness as you consider each sin, recognizing the ways it harmed you as well as your relationship with God and others. Then, knowing God wants to embrace and forgive you, confess your sins and feel God's loving response to each confession.

3.   Conclude your confession by offering a prayer of joyful trust, allowing each word and phrase to linger on your consciousness and invoke the joy and trust that you feel after restoring your relationship with love with God.

4.   Go back into your daily life, aware of God's love and protection while offering the penances that are appropriate to the sins of your confession.

Seeking Your Place of Resurrection

some final thoughts as you continue on your pilgrimage

While you have completed these reflections and exercises, your spiritual journey has not ended. Still, you may move forward with confidence knowing that you will never be alone. God's love enfolds and protects you, and you walk in the continuing presence of Christ through the grace of the Holy Spirit.

For the ancient Celtic saints, following God's desires involved an individual search for the person's "place of resurrection". From the stories you have heard during your retreat and in these reflections and exercises, you know that this quest was often taken quite literally - the individual sought that place where they could prayerfully live wholly devoted to God's presence while waiting for their death and resurrection from that specific location.

However, in our global and interconnected world, it is possible – perhaps even necessary – to reinterpret the meaning of a "place of resurrection". Instead of seeking a place where we seek to be alone with God, we should strive to find those places in our world where God's love is most needed and where we may use the unique gifts God has given to each of us to manifest God's presence in those places (see 1 Peter 4: 10), whether in service to a particular community throughout our lives or through a particular ministry in many different places.

It is possible that you have already found your own special "place of resurrection". If so, I may you find joy and satisfaction in manifesting the presence of God in your life of service and prayer. However, if you are still seeking "place of resurrection" (or you feel a need to understand God's desires in the place he has already selected for you), you might consider making a longer retreat (such as *The Spiritual Exercises of Saint Ignatius of Loyola*) after you allow adequate time for the graces of these reflections and exercises to intertwine with your being (by following the advice offered at the end of your retreat in *A Pilgrimage to the Land of the Saints*).

Whether you already have found your "place of resurrection", or are still seeking it, you also need find a spiritual guide or soul friend to help you deeper in your journey of faith. You may choose to avail yourself of the activities of SilentHeron.net, but these are not the only resources available to you. Look around you and find the people and support systems that best help you fulfill God's unique desires for you

So, as you continue your spiritual journey, may this prayer sing in your heart:

> Life be in my speech,
> sense in what I say,
> the bloom of cherries on my lips,
> till I come back again.
> The love Jesus Christ gave
> be filling every heart for me,
> the love Jesus Christ gave
> filling me for everyone.
> Traversing corries, traversing forests,
> traversing valleys long and wild,
> the Shepherd Jesus still uphold me,
> the Shepherd Jesus be my shield.

Further Reading

Further Reading

The following books were consulted when discussing Celtic spirituality in *A Journey to the Land of the Saints* and *A Pilgrimage to the Land of the Saints*:

Adam, David. *A Desert in the Ocean: God's Call to Adventurous Living*. London: Society for Promoting Christian Knowledge, 2000.

——. *The Cry of the Deer: Meditations on the Hymn of Saint Patrick*. London: Society for Promoting Christian Knowledge, 1987.

Bradley, Ian. *Celtic Christian Communities: Live the Tradition*. Kelowna, British Columbia: Northstone Publishing, 2000

——. *The Celtic Way*. London: Darton, Longman & Todd Ltd, 1993

Carmichael, Alexander (trans./ed.). *Carmina Gadelica: Hymns and Incantations Collected in the Highlands and Islands in the Last Century*. Edinburgh: Floris Books, 1994.

Colum, Padraic. *The Poet's Circuits: Collected Poems of Ireland*. Dublin: Dolmen Press, 1981.

Davies, Oliver (ed.), with the collaboration of Thomas O'Loughlin. *Celtic Spirituality*. New York: Paulist Press, 1999.

De Waal, Esther. *The Celtic Way of Prayer: the Recovery of the Religious Tradition*. New York: Image Books, 1997

——. *Every Earthly Blessing: Rediscovering the Celtic Tradition*. Harrisburg, PA: Morehouse Publishing, 1999.

MacMaster, Johnston. *A Passion for Justice: Social Ethics in the Celtic Tradition*. Edinburgh: Dunedin Academic Press Ltd., 2008,

O'Meara, John J. (trans.). *The Voyage of Saint Brendan: Journey to the Promised Land*. Gerrards Cross, Buckinghamshire, UK: Colin Smythe Limited, 1991.

Rochelle, Gabriel Cooper. *A Staff to the Pilgrim: Meditations on the Way with Nine Celtic Saints*. Emmaus, PA: Golden Alley Press, 2016.

Sellner, Edward C. *Wisdom of the Celtic Saints*. Notre Dame, IN: Ave Maria Press, 1993

Sheldrake, Philip. *Living Between Worlds: Place and Journey in Celtic Spirituality*. Boston, MA: Cowley Publications, 1995.

Stratman, Paul. *Prayers from the Ancient Celtic Church*. Scotts Valley, CA: CreateSpace Independent Publishing Platform, 2018.

Van de Weyer, Robert. *Celtic Parables: Stories, poems and prayers*. London: Society for Promoting Christian Knowledge, 2009.

If you are interested in exploring the affinities between Celtic and Ignatian spiritualities shaping the spiritual practices developed in *A Journey to the Land of the Saints* and *A Pilgrimage to the Land of the Saints*, please consult the footnotes to the reflections in the first section of *A Journey to the Land of the Saints*.

About the Author

A former Jesuit, **Timothy J. Ray** brings a diverse background in creative writing, cultural studies, theology and the history of ideas to his work in spiritual direction and formation. He received his Bachelor of Arts, *magna cum laude*, in a multi-disciplinary program focused on the cultural history of law and politics from Niagara University before earning, with distinction, both his Master of Fine Arts in Dramaturgy and Dramatic Criticism from Yale University and his Master of Letters in Theology from the University of Saint Andrews. In addition to preparing *Nurturing the Courage of Pilgrims*, he has published *A Journey to the Land of the Saints*, *A Pilgrimage to the Land of the Saints* and *The Carmichael Prayerbook*.

For more information about Timothy and his activities, please visit http://www.silentheron.net.

Printed in Great Britain
by Amazon

85009804R10071